BEIJING

smart guide

APA PUBLICATIONS

Part of the Langenscheidt Publishing Group

Contents

Areas

A–Z

Below: Chaowai SOHO in the Central Business District.

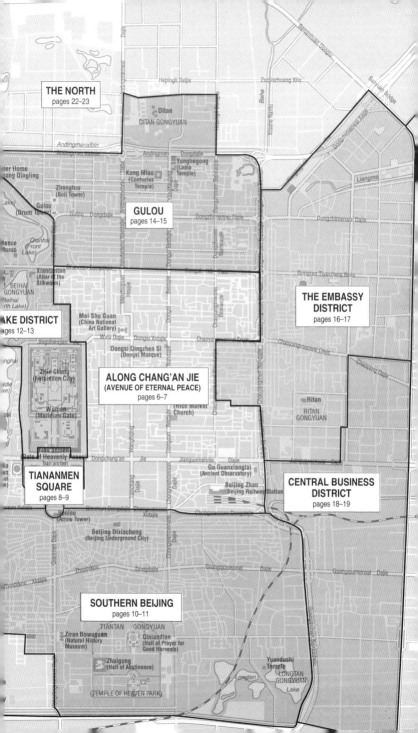

THE NORTH
pages 22–23

Hepingli Beijie

Sanyuan Bridge

Bahe

Xibahe Nanlu

Zuojiazhuang Xilu

Dongzhimenwai Xiao

Andingmenxilin

Andingmen Beijie

Andingmen

Dongdajie

Ditan
DITAN GONGYUAN

er Home
song Qingling

Zhonglou
(Bell Tower)

Kong Miao
(Confucius
Temple)

Yonghegong
(Lama
Temple)

Liangma

Gulou
(Drum Tower)

Gulou   Dongdajie

GULOU
pages 14–15

Dongzhimennei Dajie

Dongzhimenwai Dajie

ence
foruo

Qianhai
(Front
Lake)

Xiannantan
(Altar of the
Silkworm)

Baochao Dongdajie

Houhai

Jiaodaokou

Dongzhimennei Nanxiaojie

Dongsi Beidajie

Gongren Tiyuchang Beilu

**THE EMBASSY
DISTRICT**
pages 16–17

BEIHAI
GONGYUAN
orth Park)

AKE DISTRICT
ges 12–13

Jingshanqian

Mei Shu Guan
(China National
Art Gallery)

Wusi Dajie

Dongsi Xidajie

Dongsi Qingzhen Si
(Dongsi Mosque)

Chaoyang

Chaoyangmennei Dajie

Chaoyangmen Nandajie

Chaoyangmenwai Dajie

Chaoyang Dajie

Zijin Cheng
(Forbidden City)

Wumen
(Meridian Gate)

**ALONG CHANG'AN JIE
(AVENUE OF ETERNAL PEACE)**
pages 6–7

(Rice Market
Church)

Ritan

RITAN
GONGYUAN

Tian'anmen
Gate of Heavenly Peace)
Tian'anmen

Dongchang'an   Jie

Jianguomennei   Dajie

Gu Guanxiangtai
(Ancient Observatory)

**TIANANMEN
SQUARE**
pages 8–9

Beijing Zhan
(Beijing Railway Station)

**CENTRAL BUSINESS
DISTRICT**
pages 18–19

Jianguomen Nandajie

Qianmen Dongdajie   Dajie

Chongwenmen   Dongdajie

Guanghua

Jianhua

Jianlou
(Arrow Tower)

Qianmen Xidajie

Beijing Dixiacheng
(Beijing Underground City)

Tiantan   Dongdajie

Zhushikou

Zhushikou Xidajie

Dongdajie

Guangqumennei   Dajie

Guangqumenwai Dajie

Guangqumen Nandajie

SOUTHERN BEIJING
pages 10–11

TIANTAN   GONGYUAN

Ziran Bowuguan
(Natural History
Museum)

Qiniandian
(Hall of Prayer for
Good Harvests)

Zhaigong
(Hall of Abstinence)

Yuandushi
Temple

LONGTAN
GONGYUAN
Lake

Longtan

(TEMPLE OF HEAVEN PARK)

Below: People 8 Restaurant.

Beijing

The Chinese capital, Beijing, is a 21st-century city with a Ming-dynasty heart. There is a grace in its palaces and pagodas; a tang of tragedy in soldier-patrolled Tiananmen Square; and a splendour in the futuristic skyscrapers that twist its skyline. This heaving, yet ordered, metropolis is rich in history, culture and cuisines, and offers an increasingly dynamic nightlife.

Beijing Facts and Figures

Population: **17.4 million**
Area: **16,800sq km**; Tiananmen Square and the Forbidden City are slap bang in the centre, with the city divided into concentric bands by four ring roads
Location: **40°N**, same latitude as New York and Madrid
Language: **Putonghua (Mandarin Chinese)**
Climate: **continental**, with four clearly defined seasons. Summers are long and scorching; winters are long and harsh; and spring is short and prone to sandstorms. Autumn, which is warm and sunny, is the best time to visit.

Atmosphere

Beijing is a city of opposites and extremes – it captivates and confuses, excites and exasperates, all in equal measure. As the capital of the People's Republic, it is both the seat of the world's largest Communist bureaucracy and the source of the policy changes that have turned China into an economic powerhouse. Its walled compounds and towering ministries are full of bureaucrats who technically legislate in the name of Marx and Mao, while the streets outside are a riot of speeding cars, flashing neon and cell-phone-wielding citizens whose aspirations and lifestyles are increasingly akin to those of London or New York. Beijing may lack the futuristic glow of Shanghai – it remains altogether a grittier place than its southern rival – but nonetheless the changes in the past few years are remarkable.

A City of Circles

Screened from the north by a semicircle of hills, the city lies on a plain which opens out to the south. In an analogy to this position, all important buildings are built to face south, thus protecting them from the harmful *yin* influences of the north – be they the vicious Siberian winter winds or enemies from the steppes.

The sheer size of the city is overwhelming at first, yet there is order in the madness. At its heart is a giant open-air museum, the Forbidden City. Adjacent to the south is the world's largest public square, Tiananmen, with its gargantuan Communist buildings, monuments and historical gravitas. Encircling these are four concentric ring roads: the first one – called the Second Ring Road since the first one is literally the walls of the Forbidden City – marks the boundaries of the 500-year-old city wall which Mao destroyed in his spat against reminders of China's past in the 1950s. By the time you get to the Fifth Ring Road you are well into the city's suburbs – mini-satellite towns of high-rise apartments and giant warehouse shopping centres.

South of Tiananmen Square is the glorious Temple of Heaven, surrounded by its

Below: dusk falls on tranquil Kunming Lake at the New Summer Palace.

pleasant park. To the east are the shiny modern shopping centres grouped around Wangfujing, while further east you first cross the leafy Embassy District, dotted with nightclubs, bars and restaurants before it merges into the chaotic Central Business District, dominated by the Escher-twists of the new China Central Television Tower in Guanghua Street. Beijing's real gem, though, is the haven of peace in the parks and lakes area just north of the Forbidden City.

The Olympics

Beijing is in the midst of reinventing itself as it prepares to host the 2008 Summer Olympics. The games are widely seen as an unparal-

leled opportunity to sell the world its own, and China's, past greatness and future potential. Bigger and grander architectural boasts are being constructed, while fabulous old buildings are getting facelifts – or being demolished. Everything from the subway system to the air quality to the number of English-speakers is being improved – to varying degrees of success. From the builders' dust, officials hope a city with modern infrastructure and eye-popping architecture, whether young or old, will emerge.

Beijing is a city on a mad dash to the top, one can only hope that respect for the past will survive into the future as it realises its Olympic dreams.

Highlights

▲ 'You're not a real man until you've been to **The Great Wall**,' said Mao Zedong.

▶ Beijing Duck, **Peking Duck**, *kaoya*; whatever you like to call it: this crispy roasted duck is the city's namesake dish.

▲ **Tiananmen Square**, the site of numerous protests, commemorates the revolution with statues and Mao's Mausoleum.

▶ Built in 1420, the remarkable **Temple of Heaven** served as a place of ritual for Ming and Qing emperors.

▲ The **Forbidden City** functioned as the fulcrum of the ordered cosmos that was imperial China.

▶ Beijing's **nightlife** now has tones of New York. Sip a cocktail in one of its many funky lounges.

Along Chang'an Jie (Avenue of Eternal Peace)

Chang'an Jie lies along Beijing's main east–west axis and bristles with the country's icons of power – past and present. Lining its tree-lined expanse are Tiananmen Square, the Forbidden City and block after block of grand government and bank buildings, some dating back to the 1900s and interspersed with modern shopping malls and architectural experiments like Paul Andreu's National Grand Theatre. This boulevard is also the venue for mighty military parades. There is simply no other Beijing street to compare.

Jianguomen

Tucked into the top of a watchtower on the junction between the eastern edge of Chang'an Jie (here called Jianguomen) and the Second Ring Road is one of the world's oldest observatories. Stargazers from the Ming and Qing dynasties used the elaborate bronze instruments in Beijing's **Ancient Observatory** (Gu Guanxiangtai) to make predictions and advise emperors.

Heading west along the tree-lined avenue, the towers either side are a hotchpotch of traditional architecture, 1980s-style government buildings, and the glassy facades of commercial towers. Peek south when you reach the horseshoe-shaped Beijing International Hotel for the **Beijing Station**, which blends traditional architecture with the severe lines of 1950s Communist planning.
SEE ALSO TRANSPORT, P.127

Wangfujing

Wangfujing is the capital's premier shopping street, and its premier shopping mall is Hong Kong tycoon Li Kai-shing's gigantic pink **Oriental Plaza**. The street, pedestrianised as far up as Dong'anmen, is a great place to stroll, window-shop and people-watch. Halfway up on the right-hand side is the pocket-sized grey-brick **St Joseph's** ①, also called the East Cathedral, which holds a lively Sunday Mass. As dusk falls, stall-owners in the nearby **Dong'anmen Night Market** ② fire up their woks; expect the cheekier chefs to waggle snakes on a stick at the foreigners. At the northern end of Wangfujing is the **National Art Museum** ③, which periodically has some great exhibitions.

A taste of colonial-era Beijing can be found back on Chang'an Jie. Opposite the Oriental Plaza is the **Beijing Hotel**. The central part, which dates back to the early 1900s and was built in the French colonial style, is now home to the ever-elegant **Raffles Beijing Hotel**. On the southern side of the avenue is the entrance to Beijing's **Foreign Legation Quarter** ④, where European powers were grudgingly permitted to establish concessions after the Second Opium War. While most of the buildings have been taken over by the government, the area is well worth strolling through; the villas and man-

Catch a bird's-eye view of Chang'an Jie from the 28th-floor revolving restaurant in the **Beijing International Hotel**. It takes two hours to sweep through the whole panorama from Tiananmen to the Central Business District towards the east. *See also Hotels, p.60*

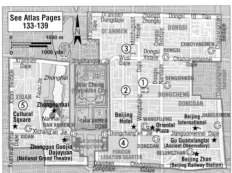

Left: the wide expanse of Chang'an Jie.

during the 1989 Tiananmen Square protests.

Continuing west, the next set of rich red palace walls hides the **Zhongnanhai** leadership compound, the seat of the politburo and the state council since 1949. Don't get your hopes up: common folk are not admitted into this modern-day Forbidden City unless they are invited. Opposite, and clashing in true modern Beijing fashion, is the **National Grand Theatre**, a dramatic titanium-and-glass dome dubbed 'The Egg'.
SEE ALSO ARCHITECTURE, P.31;
MUSIC, DANCE AND THEATRE, P.78;
PALACES AND HOMES, P.86

Xidan ⑤

The commercial craziness of **Xidan** wraps up the western end of Chang'an Jie. Beijing's teens flock here at weekends for cheap and trendy fashions; there are half a dozen or more multi-storey shopping malls branching out from the landscaped **Xidan Culture Square**. Of most interest to foreigners are the **Beijing Books Building** (its basement has a good selection of English-language titles) and the **Science and Technology Mall**.
SEE ALSO LITERATURE, P.73;
SHOPPING, P.112

sions remain ensconced in hushed tree-lined streets, a world away from the crowded, jostling arteries of downtown Beijing. The former American Legation, in the far southwest corner, has been morphed into a funky restaurant, bar and art-gallery complex complete with an underground theatre. It's due to open in 2008.
SEE ALSO HOTELS, P.61; SHOPPING,
P.111–12, 113; TEMPLES,
CHURCHES AND MOSQUES, P.118

Tiananmen Gate

By the time you reach Mao's portrait you are at the symbolic centre and political heart of Beijing. To the south is **Tiananmen Square** (see p.8–9), while to the north, through the **Gate of Heavenly Peace** (Tiananmen Gate) is the **Forbidden City** (Gu Gong). This ancient palace was the hallowed nucleus of the Chinese empire for nearly five centuries.

Mao's portrait measures 6m (19ft) by 4.5m (14.5 ft) and weighs 1.5 tonnes; it is cleaned before Labour Day (1 May) and replaced before National Day (1 Oct), when Mao is joined by the founder of the Republic, Sun Yat-sen. Multiple copies of the portrait are kept in case of vandalism: disgruntled Chinese periodically throw paint or soot at Mao. Journalist Yu Dongyue was sentenced to more than 16 years for pelting the portrait with red-paint-filled eggshells

Right: Oriental Plaza.

Tiananmen Square

This giant open space at Beijing's heart, where imperial and Communist monuments meet, reflects China's tumultuous history. It is to this immense plaza – said to be the world's largest public square – that visitors to the Chinese capital are initially drawn. Imperial gateways face the monuments and museums erected by the Communist regime that flank the square. For many Westerners, the words 'Tiananmen Square' have become synonymous with the democracy demonstrations of 1989, and their brutal suppression; but on a daily basis the square functions as a concrete park, complete with kite-flyers and picnickers.

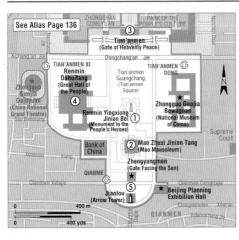

See Atlas Page 136

Tiananmen Square started out as a T-shaped corridor during the Qing dynasty. In 1911 it was opened to the public and began its life as the place to air grievances. May the Fourth protesters gathered here in 1919. In the late 1950s the square was quadrupled in size and paved with concrete so that it could accommodate up to a million people. Near-hysterical gatherings of Red Guards were a regular sight here when the Cultural Revolution broke out in the mid-1960s. And 20 years on the world watched as students staged mass democracy protests in the face of army tanks in the summer of 1989.

The Square

In the middle of the square is the **Monument to the People's Heroes** ① (Renmin Yinxiong Jinian Bei), an obelisk dedicated in 1958 to the remembrance of soldiers who fell in the civil war. To the north is the national flag, which to great ceremony and crowds of sightseers, is raised without fail at dawn and likewise lowered at dusk. To the south is the **Mao Mausoleum** ② (Mao Zhuxi Jinian Tang, Tues–Sun 8am–noon, free), where the wizened, embalmed body of the Great Helmsman is on view in a crystal coffin. There is a theory that Mao himself wanted to be cremated. The group sculptures by the front and rear entrances to the mausoleum, depicting the people's struggle for social-ism, are typical examples of socialist realism. The square is serviced by two ridiculously close subway stops, East and West Tiananmen on the res-pective corners of the plaza.

Gate of Heavenly Peace

At the northern end of Tianan-men Square, across the 38m-(125ft-) wide Chang'an Jie, seven marble bridges lead across a small moat to the **Gate of Heavenly Peace** ③ (Tiananmen Gate). Mao pro-claimed the People's Republic of China from this spot on 1 Oct 1949, and in the same way received the adulation of millions of Red Guards during the Cultural Revolution. To the left of Mao's portrait is a sign in Chinese characters: 'Long live the People's Republic of China.' The sign on the right says, 'Long live the great unity of all the peoples of the world.'

Communist Behemoths

Vast Soviet-style edifices flank the east and west sides of the square. **The Great Hall of the**

1 - 14 PROB OV

9 - 7 PROBS

6 - 15 USER

Left: Tiananmen, a traditional place of protests, is well guarded.

Mao's status in 21st-century China is odd – he is at once the father of the nation and the man who, in the official words of the Party, got it '70 percent right and 30 percent wrong'; still revered as something like a god by many, yet his image has been removed from public display throughout the land – the portrait at Tiananmen being the one exception. Ironically, his image still appears on all bank-notes. The rapid rise of the Mao memorabilia phenomenon further muddies the waters.

People ④ (Renmin Dahui-tang), on the west side, is open daily except when in session. The National People's Assembly, the Chinese parliament, meets in the 50,000sq-m building. There isn't much to see, but walking around the dimly lit, cavernous halls with their red carpets, overbearing Chinese art and polished wooden floors certainly gives a feel of the Party spirit.

Directly opposite the Great Hall of the People is the **National Museum of China** (Zhongguo Guojia Bowuguan), which, unfortunately, is closed for extensive revamping and will not be open until 2010. Many of its 620,000 pieces are being lent out to the **Capital Museum** (see p.77).

Qianmen

At the southern end of Tiananmen Square, **Qian-** **men** ⑤ (Front Gate) was once the outer, southern entrance into the old Inner (Chinese) City from the Outer (Tartar) City, and dates from 1421. The gate is in fact comprised of two separate structures; the stone **Jianlou** (Arrow Tower), which burned down in 1900 and was reconstructed in 1903; and the main gate, the wooden **Zhengyangmen** (Gate Facing the Sun), just to the north, also damaged in 1900 and reconstructed, to which the city wall was connected. For a small fee you can climb Zhengyangmen and survey the whole square; Mao's portrait appears postage-stamp-sized in the distance.

The **Beijing Planning Exhibition Hall**, just west of Qianmen, has displays that illustrate 3,000 years of the city's history and a vision of its future. Don a pair of binoculars and scan the mammoth surreal model from above.

SEE MUSEUMS AND GALLERIES, P.76

Right: the Monument to the People's Heroes.

Southern Beijing

The southern part of the city is undergoing radical and controversial reconstruction. Its oldest thoroughfare is being recreated as it was 100 years ago, with trolley buses and old-style shopfronts. Much of the surrounding labyrinth of shabby hutong has now been bulldozed. A few key lanes remain, though, conjuring up the past with ancient teashops, pharmacies and shoemakers. Tourist-built handicraft districts, opera theatres, a hefty pearl market and some of the city's finest Beijing duck restaurants are other reasons to head down this way. The premier attraction is at the Temple of Heaven, with its complex of indigo prayer halls set in the grounds of a wonderful park.

Qianmen Dajie ①

Qianmen Dajie, which runs along the city's ancient north–south axis, is undergoing a major facelift. Work is scheduled to be finished by mid-2008. Authorities are promising something of the flavour of the major commercial highway of Qianmen's Qing-dynasty days, complete with working trams and moats, although minus the opium dens and brothels. **Quanjude**, the original Peking duck restaurant that has been roasting birds since 1864, was rebuilt in the revamp. The restaurant was forced to close, but its wood fires were kept burning even though there were no customers –

Tongrentang is reputed to be the oldest Chinese medicine shop in the country, founded back in 1669. The apothecary has not survived, but flourished – it now has branches throughout China, around Asia, and even in such far-off places as London and Sydney.

they have never been allowed to go out since the restaurant first opened. **Beijing's Underground City** (Dixia Cheng), is a small hutong to the east, is a network of tunnels and bunkers built amid fears of Soviet attack following the 1960 bust-up between the two countries. It's a venture into the bizarre – the dripping tunnels are home to gas-mask-wearing dummies, all manner of junk and an incongruous Chinese products emporium.

Dazhalan is a bustling, twisting hutong heading west from Qianmen Dajie that is famous for its old shops and businesses.

SEE ALSO RESTAURANTS, P.100; SHOPPING, P.110–11

Liulichang

Further to the west through the maze of hutong is **Liulichang**, meaning literally 'glazed tile factory', a shopping street restored in the 1980s to its original style, which offers a wide range of Chinese arts and crafts with a generous helping of kitsch.

Left: hutong, and their traditions, face a battle of survival.

ing Heaven, gathers around one of the most impressive buildings in China, the **Hall of Prayer for Good Harvests**. The southern group, meanwhile, has a square layout that symbolises Earth. Come early in the morning before the tour groups arrive.

SEE ALSO TEMPLES, CHURCHES AND MOSQUES, P.118–19

A Step away from Heaven

Beijing's **Natural History Museum** ③ (Ziran Bowuguan) is in an ivy-clad building just to the west of the Temple of Heaven. There is also an entertaining collection of animatronic dinosaurs in the poorly lit basement, which growl and bellow at passers-by, sometimes in Mandarin.

Just across the street from the Temple of Heaven's east gate, and reached via a footbridge, is an ugly twin-towered building housing the ever-popular **Hongqiao Market** ④. Clothes, shoes, watches and fake designer goods are sold on the first and second floors, antiques, silk and – emphatically – pearls on the second and third. Head to the fifth floor for some good views of the Temple of Heaven.

SEE ALSO MUSEUMS AND GALLERIES, P.76; SHOPPING, P.112

Critics of the destruction of Beijing's **hutong** have reserved particular anger for the razing of the old Qianmen courtyards. Because of its central location, the land is invaluable to property developers. Hundreds of families have been forced out of their homes to make way for commercial property, blocks of soulless flats and a sprinkling of renovated million-dollar courtyard homes for the rich. Admittedly much of the area was a slum, but critics wanted the government to modernise and clean it up without demolishing the hutong and throwing the original families out.

See also Hutong, p.68–9.

Its name derives from the Ming-dynasty kilns built nearby to provide glazed tiles for the new Imperial Palace.

A short distance to the north and tucked in a hutong is the **Zhengyici Beijing Opera Theatre**, the oldest

Beijing Opera theatre, constructed entirely of wood around 350 years ago. It is a beautiful setting in which to see performances. A 10-minute walk south, the **Huguang Guildhall**, on Hufang Qiao, is another atmospheric place to see opera in the city. There is also a small museum on site.

SEE ALSO BEIJING OPERA, P.35; SHOPPING, P.111

Temple of Heaven ②

The spectacular **Temple of Heaven** (Tiantan) complex, a good 25-minute walk south down Qianmen Dajie, is set in the middle of one of the city's most visited parks, alive at all hours with residents practising opera and t'ai chi. The buildings of the temple are divided into two main groups: northern and southern. The northern group, built to a semicircular layout represent-

Right: underground chic.

The Lake District

The area immediately north and west of the Forbidden City is the most untouched part of Beijing, a patchwork of lakes and parks, once pleasure grounds of the imperial family and spread with fish ponds, pavilions, Buddhist temples and rock gardens. While rampant commercial development around the lakes at Qianhai and Houhai has spoiled them somewhat, the area retains much of its historical flavour, and there are nooks to discover around the back of old hutong where important figures in Chinese history lived in graceful mansions. Ignore the neon and it is easy to imagine the lake in imperial times.

Zhongshan Park

The Forbidden City is surrounded on three sides by parks – a fusion of imperial architecture and design. To the west, **Zhongshan Park** ①

(Zhongshan Gongyuan) is notable for its cypresses, the remains of a sacrificial altar, a wooden prayer hall and the **Forbidden City Concert Hall**, which puts on concerts.

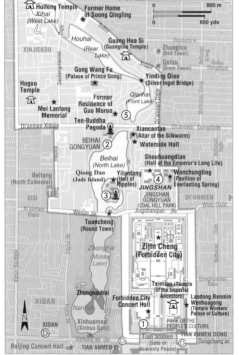

To the east is the **Workers' Palace of Culture** (Laodong Renmin Wenhuagong). In the centre of the complex is the **Taimiao** (Imperial Ancestral Temple), where ancestor worship rituals took place.

SEE ALSO MUSIC, DANCE AND THEATRE, P.78; PARKS AND GARDENS, P.99; TEMPLES, CHURCHES AND MOSQUES, P.120

Beihai Park

Beihai Park ② (Beihai Gongyuan) is one of the most beautiful and popular places to spend a day, no matter the season. In winter, the lake is used for skating; during the rest of the year, everyone goes boating. **Jade Island** (Hortensia Island or Qiong Dao) is the most impressive part of the park as far as scenery and history are concerned. Visible from most parts of central Beijing is the 35m (115ft) **White Dagoba** ③, an onion-shaped shrine in the Tibetan style,

Left: Yinding Bridge.

The back lakes are a favourite haunt of rickshaw drivers, who hassle anyone who looks remotely like a tourist to take their hutong tour. The price is around 180 yuan for two hours; and while it's a fun way to see the lanes, be prepared for plenty of stops along the way to souvenir emporiums. A highlight is the *siheyuan* experience, a chance to take tea with a family in their courtyard home.

built on the ruins of a Ming palace in honour of the fifth Dalai Lama's visit to Beijing in 1651. Next door, in the **Hall of Ripples** (Yilamtang), is the **Fangshan Restaurant** established in 1925 by chefs of the imperial household who were suddenly left unemployed when Pu Yi was forced out of the Imperial Palace in 1924.

The other part of the lake, **Zhongnanhai** (Central and Southern Lake) was a pleasure garden for the court. Now it is the seat of government and is off limits.

SEE ALSO PARKS AND GARDENS, P.96; RESTAURANTS, P.102

Jingshan (Coal Hill)

Directly behind the Forbidden City is **Jingshan** ④ (Coal Hill), an artificial hill built at the beginning of the 15th century from the dirt dug out to make the moats surrounding the Forbidden City. The view from the **Pavilion of Everlasting Spring** (Wanchungting), on the middle of five peaks, is superb. The **Hall of the Emperor's Long Life** (Shouhuangdian) is where corpses of empresses were laid before being removed to tombs outside the city.

SEE ALSO PARKS AND GARDENS, P.98

The Lakes

The lakes north of Beihai Park are home to beautiful courtyard palaces of Manchu princes and Qing-dynasty officials. Unfortunately, in recent years developers have been given free rein to ruin; the main stretch of neon

Left: Lotus Lane at night.

glare is **Lotus Lane** ⑤, a pedestrian-only area on the southwestern shore of **Qianhai Lake**. A popular nightlife area is concentrated around little **Yinding Qiao** (Silver Ingot Bridge), where **Houhai Lake** meets Qianhai.

Nearby on Qianhai Xijie is the **Guo Moruo's Former Residence**, an influential figure in the rise of Communism in China, and a short walk north is the **Palace of Prince Gong** (Gong Wang Fu), a very popular destination for tour groups. A slight detour to the west is the **Mei Lanfang Memorial**, dedicated to the man who is China's most celebrated Beijng Opera performer. The nearby **Mei Mansion** is an elegant restaurant that cooks up the opera stars' favourite dishes.

Beyond the Yinding Bridge, on the east bank of Houhai, is the **Guang Hua Si** (Guanghua Temple). Constructed during the Yuan dynasty, this active temple is now home to the Beijing Buddhist Society. The **Soong Qingling's Former Home** is nearby on the western bank of Houhai.

SEE ALSO BEIJING OPERA, P.34; PALACES AND HOMES, P.90; RESTAURANTS, P.103; TEMPLES, CHURCHES AND MOSQUES, P.119–20

Gulou

The area east of Houhai Lake has some of the city's finest hutong. The web of tree-lined lanes offers a glimpse into the traditional lives of ordinary Beijingers – red-painted doorways, men playing chess, fortune tellers and dodgy hairdressers. Spliced with this is an array of cafés, courtyard restaurants, curious bars and gift shops. While popular with tourists and resident expatriates, locals tend to outnumber the foreigners here. Come summertime, a night-time cycle around this maze is magical. The area also boasts two imposing towers dating from the rule of Kublai Khan, a massive Tibetan temple, and a Ming-dynasty university complete with a moat-encircled lecture hall.

Bell and Drum Towers

During the period of Mongol rule, the **Bell** (Gulou) ① and **Drum** (Zhonglou) ② **towers** stood at the centre of the capital, then known as Dadu. In the Ming dynasty they were rebuilt a little east of their original position. Climb the Drum Tower's steep staircase of 69 steps for an unmatched view of a disappearing old-style neighbourhood. Looking down upon the grey and often grass-covered tile roofs, separated into a variety of geometric shapes by the walls of the hutong, you can get a sense of how each siheyuan courtyard is a community in itself. The public square

Above: no amateur rhythms allowed at the Drum Tower.

between the two towers is popular with families at night walking their dogs and playing ball games with their children.

Nanluogu Xiang

Unlike Houhai, which has been more or less killed by over-commercialisation, **Nanluogu Xiang** ③, a major hutong dotted with cute wi-fi cafés and restaurants, has been tastefully developed. From the Drum Tower head east along **Gulou Dongdajie**, a busy tree-lined street packed with musical instrument shops and boutiques, for about five minutes. The lane, which is marked, is on the right-hand side opposite the **Huangwa Temple**, a yellow-tiled Daoist hall to the God of Wealth. It is worthwhile exploring the hutong branching off Nanluo and

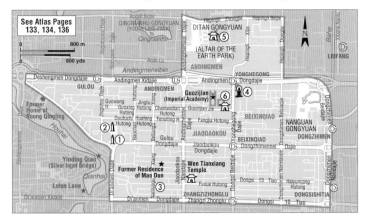

Left: Lama Temple

Temple ⑥ (Kong Miao) and the adjoining **Imperial Academy** (Guozijian). One of the most impressive sights in the temple are the 198 stone tablets recording the names and hometowns of 51,624 candidates who successfully passed imperial exams during the Yuan, Ming and Qing dynasties. Guozijian churned out tens of thousands of scholars for the emperor's court. Guozijian Jie is fast becoming a Nanluogu Xiang hopeful, with its own army of kooky little cafés and bars. There is also a well-established vegetarian restaurant, **Xu Xiang Zhai**, popular with monks.

SEE ALSO RESTAURANTS, P.104; TEMPLES, CHURCHES AND MOSQUES, P.120–1

Gulou Dongdajie; there are a plethora of little courtyard restaurants and hideaway bars here.

Lama Temple

Further to the east is the **Lama Temple** ④ (Yonghegong, Palace of Eternal Harmony), a series of five impressive Tibetan prayer halls that date back to 1694, when the complex formed part of the city wall. More than 70 brown-robed monks now live here. The temple belongs to the Yellow Hat or Gelugpa sect of Buddhism, whose spiritual head is the Dalai Lama.

SEE ALSO TEMPLES, CHURCHES AND MOSQUES, P.121–2

Ditan Park

Across the busy Second Ring Road is **Ditan Park** (Ditan Gongyuan), which spreads around the **Altar of the Earth** ⑤, one of the original eight altars, along with the Temple of Heaven, that played a great role in the ritual life of the Ming and Qing emperors.

SEE ALSO PARKS AND GARDENS, P.97

Confucius Temple

Across the road from the Lama Temple, **Guozijian Jie** is graced by two of only a few existing *pailou* (decorative gates) left standing in Beijing. Halfway down on the right-hand side are the **Confucius**

The current **Dalai Lama**, the 14th, lives in exile in India; he fled Tibet from invading Chinese soldiers in 1959 and has been a thorn in Beijing's side ever since. As he is now well into his 70s, the issue of his successor has become more urgent. Atheist Beijing is adamant that only the party has the power to name the next spiritual head of Tibet; something which will not sit well with Tibetans. In summer 2007, Beijing banned reincarnations of 'living Buddhas' that do not have government approval, effectively usurping any decision from the Dalai Lama. In the meantime, Tibet's spiritual leader has come up with no clear plan. In 2007 he made various surprising suggestions, including holding a referendum to see whether a new Dalai Lama is necessary, or choosing a successor himself before he dies. He even said the next Dalai Lama might be a woman.

Right: newly-weds head to Ditan Park for a photo shoot.

The Embassy District

E astern Beijing has long been the city's international district, home to scores of embassies and the diplomats who staff them. Sections retain the flavour of the 1980s, when foreigners shopped in Friendship Stores and lived in special compounds. Many travellers today end up staying here, in a gleaming high-rise hotel where English is the official language and a Starbucks is certain to be just around the corner. While the bulk of the capital's bars, clubs, restaurants and Western-style shopping malls are also here, there are pockets of intrigue – a grungy Russian quarter with warehouses and fur shops, a pagoda-filled park, and a couple of curious temples.

Jianguomen Diplomatic Quarter

The leafy lanes of the **Jianguomen Diplomatic Quarter**, with embassies set behind high walls and guarded by soldiers, are an oasis of peace from the neon bars and clubs a few blocks north. To the south, on Jianguomenwai Dajie is the overpriced **Youyi Shangdian** (Friendship Store), while just to the northwest is **Yabao Lu** ①, or the Russian quarter, popular with the Uigher minority from China's northwest Xinjiang region as well as Russian traders. You are just as likely to see signs in Cyrillic here as in Chinese. Two big malls, the bizarrely named **Alien Street Market** (formerly the Russian Market) and **M.E.N.**, sell many of the fake products popular in Silk Street *(see p.112)* but at better prices. The heart of the quarter is **Ritan** ② (Altar of the Sun), one of the eight altars which, along with the Temple of Heaven *(see p.118–19)*, played a great role in the ritual life of the Ming and Qing emperors.

SEE ALSO PARKS AND GARDENS, P.99

Below: 3.3 on Sanlitun has five floors of funky boutiques.

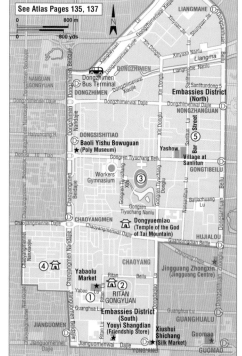

Left: another quiet day in the Diplomatic Quarter.

Sanlitun

Further north is **Sanlitun** ⑤, a street of bars and restaurants and a staunch favourite of expats. The most popular bar strip, a narrow, raucous street known as South Sanlitun, was knocked down in 2005, but the larger neighbourhood has continued to grow in popularity, although not much in class – a branch of **Hooters** opened here in 2007. The developers, though, have their eye on the region – a trio of property firms are in the process of building mega-malls which will eradicate forever its hole-in-the-wall drinking-dive reputation. The most ambitious, the **Village at Sanlitun**, which its developer Hong Kong's Swire Properties likes to call 'the capital's cosmopolitan centrepiece', will feature bars, restaurants, a boutique hotel and a cinema. It is scheduled to open in 2008. **Yashow** is an old tourist favourite stuffed with Chinese souvenirs and fake brand clothing.

SEE ALSO BARS AND CAFÉS, P.33; SHOPPING, P.112–13

Workers Stadium

The **Workers Stadium** ③ (Gongren Tiyu Chang, or Gongti for short), a 72,000-seat sports arena – down for Olympic football events – has been eclipsed by the bars and restaurants that have mushroomed along three of its four sides. The western and northern sides are home to megaclubs, while the eastern edge is more about fine dining.

A couple of blocks south is **Dongyuemiao** ③ (Temple of the God of Tai Mountain) a Daoist place of worship. **Yueshow Clothing Market**, next door, is a copy of Yashow (see right), but without the tourist hordes. A slight detour west across the Second Ring Road on Lumicang Hutong is **Zhihuasi** ④ (Temple of Perfect Wisdom), originally the family shrine of a corrupt Ming-dynasty eunuch named Wang Zhen. The temple is home to the **Ancient Music Centre**, a good place to catch Ming-dynasty ritual music.

SEE ALSO MUSIC, DANCE AND THEATRE, P.78; TEMPLES, CHURCHES AND MOSQUES, P.122

Every major Chinese city had a Friendship Store *(Youyi Shangdian)* back in the 1980s. Only foreigners, initially, could buy goods there, and they were the only places to buy Western groceries like cheese and luxury products. All that has changed now, and there are scores of shops around town catering to foreign customers. While certainly not the place to find a bargain, the store in Jianguomen sells a wide range of produce from dried mushrooms to exquisite *cloisonné*. There is a large carpet section, a stock of good silk, tailors, a bookshop, a teashop, a supermarket, and a Starbucks.

Further east, past the Third Ring Road are several areas that have become popular dining spots and watering holes, mainly due to the growth in foreign expatriates living in the city. **Chaoyang Park West Gate** has the notorious **Suzie Wong's** bar and the glitzy **Block 8** complex; **Lucky Street** (Haoyun Jie) and **Super Bar Street** (Xingba Lu) are scruffier stretches of novelty spots; while **Lido**, not far from the Shunyi expat housing development, has more family-oriented venues. *See also Nightlife, p.82–3.*

Central Business District

There is no other place in Beijing which embodies the capital's hopes of becoming a leading world city like the Central Business District. Billions of dollars have been poured into making this a jungle of skyscrapers, luxurious hotels and hot commercial property. There are towers that crave the sky, such as the 330m-high China World Trade Centre III, or vie for the curious: take the Escher-twists of the China Central Television Tower, for example. Aside from a glimpse of the future Beijing, the CBD is well worth a trek out for its antiques and curio markets and a spread of top eateries and chilled cocktail lounges. This is where the money is, after all.

Guomao

The core of the Central Business District is **Guomao**. It all started back in the 1990s with the glass horseshoe of the **China World Trade Centre** ①. It now houses Shangri-La's swanky **China World Hotel**. Just behind is the steel spike of the third phase of the project; when finished, **China World Trade Centre III** will be

Beijing's tallest building at 330m (1,083ft).

Now more than 120 Fortune 500 companies have offices in the CBD, including Samsung, Ford and Time Warner. Across Jianguomenwai Dajie, the **Yintai Centre** rivals for the skies. The 66-storey centre building, which will house the ridiculously luxurious **Park Hyatt**, will be capped with a glowing giant glass lantern. Behind is the **Jianwai Soho** complex, a playground of cream-coloured towers with boutiques, cafés, bars and restaurants that have never quite taken off.
SEE ALSO HOTELS, P.65, 66

Guanghua Lu

Head north along the Third Ring Road for this broad street, which has been

Beijing is rife with fake antiques, but if you land with the real thing note that anything made before 1840 cannot legally be exported. Many date from the early 20th century, which covers the final period of the Qing dynasty and the early Republic. Factories are constantly churning out replicas of antiques, and it is harder these days to find really beautiful pieces.

caked in dust for the past few years from being the epicentre of new construction. Across the highway is an exercise in avant-garde with the glass lego-loop of Rem Koolhaas's **CCTV**. The five-tower **Fortune Plaza** and the older, lower-level **Kerry Centre** ② – home of the infamous **Centro** cocktail lounge – offer more five-

antiques – more than 3,000 dealers offering a vast array of goods; scroll paintings, porcelain, silk, leather puppets, lacquerware and Mao memorabilia are in abundance. This is a good place to buy antiques such as old mah-jong sets, antique clocks, watches and gramophone players. Prices can be low if you bargain hard. It's now open daily, but is more lively at the weekends. If you're in the market for antique furniture, head for **Gaobeidian Furniture Street**, outside the Fourth Ring Road. While dealers say around 95 percent are fakes, if the workmanship is good that Qing-dynasty-style opium bed or painted Tibetan chest may just be worth it.
SEE ALSO SHOPPING, P.112

star hotels and fine dining. But perhaps the most playful project is **The Place** ③ on Dongdaiqiao Lu – twin shopping malls joined by a piazza and roofed with a giant digital screen. The trippy movies beamed off the ceiling make this a fun place for a prostrate late-night beer. The basement of the southernmost mall has an international spread of cuisines – there is everything from Singaporean to German to Macanese on

offer. At the southern end of Dongdaqiao is the legendary **Silk Street Market** ④ (Xiu Shui), offering a range of GoreTex jackets, Hugo Boss coats, and other brand-name clothing (much of it fake) at rock-bottom prices. The four-storey emporium also has money changers.
SEE ALSO ARCHITECTURE, P.31; BARS, P.33; HOTELS, P.65–6; SHOPPING, P.112, 113

Panjiayuan

Further south, next to Longtan Gongyuan and close to the Third Ring Road, is **Panjiayuan Market** ⑤ (Ghost Market), also sometimes known as the Dirt Market. Formerly a small gathering of merchants selling goods of variable quality, it has expanded into a sprawling showcase of Chinese and ethnic crafts and

Left: the CWTC was one of Beijing's first upmarket shopping malls.

While business executives in the West rail against the plethora of fake goods produced in China, foreign tourists flock to markets like **Silk Street** specifically to buy knock-offs. They are infinitely cheaper and look like the real thing. Who cares if they don't last as long? While no serious threat as yet to the counterfeit goods industry, Chinese authorities have been making small attempts to appear to be cracking down on the pirates. Since Silk Street is the most infamous, police periodically raid the stalls, seizing goods. Five western brands – Gucci, Chanel, Burberry, Prada and Louis Vuitton – successfully sued the market's management in 2006 for selling copies of their brands. The market was fined about US$12,000. Despite a grand relaunch in which they pledged to crack down on fakes, the knock-offs are still very much there.

Western Beijing

Asmidge off the tourist trail and often overlooked, this part of the capital holds some of its best-kept secrets. The streets have a more relaxed and local feel. This is also the religious quarter – here you will find the city's main mosque, cathedrals, one of the few working Daoist temples, Buddhist temples, and a Tibetan-Buddhist shrine designed by a Nepalese architect. The western fringes are marked by the feisty megaliths of Financial Street, a patch of five-star hotels, bank buildings and insurance towers. Choose between noodles at street level or a champagne brunch at the InterContinental Financial Street. Western Beijing has it all.

Xicheng

Xicheng means West City, but you are still well within Central Beijing here. Just a few streets west of Beihai Park, in a side hutong, is the imposing Gothic-style **North Cathedral** (Beitang), built by Jesuits in 1889. Make a dog-leg turn west and head down the main road. Opposite the

Geological Museum of China ① – marked by an incongruous giant dinosaur statue – is **Guangjisi** (Temple of Universal Rescue), a well-used and atmospheric Buddhist temple. Continue west for about five minutes for the newly restored **Lidai Diwang Miao** (Temple of Past Emperors), where emperors once

came to make sacrifices. You'll see the squat white dome, called a dagoba, of the Tibetan-style **Baitasi** (Temple of the White Pagoda) before you reach it. The **Former Residence of Lu Xun**, one of China's most influential and famous writers of the 20th century, is around the corner between Baitasi and the Second Ring Road. Though there's not much to see there is an attached bookshop selling English translations of his short stories and essays.
SEE ALSO MUSEUMS AND GALLERIES, P.77; TEMPLES, CHURCHES AND MOSQUES, P.123, 124

Financial Street

Burrow through the hutong west of here and you'll emerge in Financial Street, a cluster of skyscrapers and top business

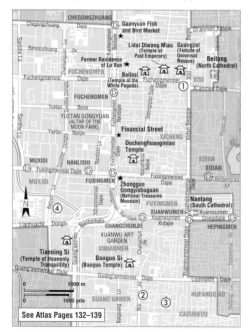

Below: fresh pickings from Guanyuan Fish and Bird Market.

Left: Hui Muslims are descendants of Central Asian traders.

ple in the inner city of Beijing, **Fayuansi** ③ (Temple of the Source of Buddhist Teaching). The temple houses the **Buddhist Academy** and is devoted to the teaching and study of Buddhism, and trains young monks for four to five years before they can enter other monasteries in China.

To the northwest, in an unpromising area dominated by thundering traffic and tower blocks, is one of the few Daoist temples left in Beijing, **Baiyunguan** ④ (Temple of the White Cloud). Used as a factory during the Cultural Revolution, the temple was restored to its original purpose and today is home to around 70-odd monks – easily identified by their white stockings and top-knotted hair.

SEE ALSO TEMPLES, CHURCHES AND MOSQUES, P.122–3, 124

hotels, such as the **InterContinental**. Currently about 1km square, the area is due for major enlargement. There are also plans, bizarrely, to build a giant underground road network with traffic lights beneath the towers; Beijing is hoping to transform the area into China's Wall Street. For now, at least, there's a vestige of the old Beijing in the **Guanyuan Fish and Bird Market** jammed into a jumble of narrow lanes just southwest of Chegongzhuang subway stop. This is the place to buy traditional wooden bird cages, singing crickets and pairs of wrinkled walnut shells (used as exercise balls for the hands).

SEE ALSO HOTELS, P.66

Of the 10 Muslim groups in China, the Hui are the most numerous at around 10 million. They are often described as Muslim with Chinese characteristics.

South of Fuximingmen

Sites in this part of the city are spread out, but within a kilometre or so of each other you can find the key religious centres for the capital's Daoists, Buddhists and Muslims. Just east of the Xuanwumen subway stop is Beijing's oldest extant church, **South Cathedral** (Nantang), founded at the beginning of the Qing dynasty, although the current structure dates from 1904.

The largest concentration of Hui (Han Chinese Muslims) in Beijing – an estimated 10,000 or more – is along Niu Jie and in its little side streets and hutong. The recently restored **Niu Jie Mosque** ②, with its curved eaves and colourfully painted support beams, looks more like a Chinese temple than a Muslim place of worship.

Just to the east, on **Fayuansi Qianjie** (a hutong leading off Niu Jie), is what is thought to be the oldest tem-

Chinese have been keeping **crickets** since the 7th century. One variety is prized for its voice, another for its ferocity. Singing crickets, once kept as inspiration for poets or carried in the pocket as buzzing pets, are regularly entered into contests – the louder and deeper the voice the better. The smaller, darker, angrier kind are bred as fighters; gambling on backstreet cricket boxing is big business. A single insect can cost several thousand yuan; that's a lot for a creature with a lifespan of around 100 days. You can pick up your own pet cricket at Guanyuan Market for around 30 yuan and also buy him a hollowed-out gourd cricket capsule with mesh ventilation holes – they even have ones painted with the face of Che Guevara. Feed him on carrot and tofu.

The North

The north has long been the home of intellectuals. Most of the city's institutes of higher learning are in the Haidian district; the older established colleges are set in stunning grounds. This concentration of minds has led to the development of Zhongguancun nearby, billed as 'China's Silicon Valley'; while the availability of open space has blessed the area with the bulk of Olympic venues, including the National Stadium and National Aquatics Centre. Further north, past the big ghostly satellite towns, are hot spring resorts. The capital's artists, meanwhile, have spread their easels in the northeast to create several funky gallery districts in abandoned factories.

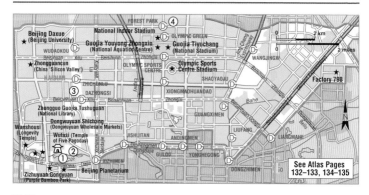

Xizhimen

Just west of Xizhimen is the **Beijing Zoo** ① (Beijing Dongwuyuan). While conditions for most of the animal inmates are Victorian and depressing, the zoo does have giant pandas. Behind is the **Beijing Aquarium** ②, which include a coral reef and sharks, seals and dolphins. Opposite the zoo is the newly pimped-out **Beijing Planetarium**, while further west along Xizhimenwai Dajie are the **Dongwuyuan Wholesale Markets**, with some of the best bargains in town for clothes. **Wutasi** (Temple of Five Pagodas), just behind the zoo, dates back to the 15th century and is quite different from other temples in Beijing.

Most impressive is a series of bas-reliefs on the outside, depicting Buddha figures and religious symbols.

Across Baishiqiao to the west is the **Purple Bamboo Park** (Zizhuyuan Gongyuan). Around its three lakes are 10 different varieties of bamboo – a rare plant in northern China. The Buddhist

Wanshousi (Longevity Temple), built in 1577, features a fine collection of bronze statues, ceramics and various other ancient artefacts. A little north, the enormous **National Library of China** (Zhongguo Guojia Tushuguan), is the largest library in Asia with some 21 million items.

SEE ALSO CHILDREN, P.38; MUSEUMS AND GALLERIES, P.77; PARKS AND GARDENS, P.99; TEMPLES, CHURCHES AND MOSQUES, P.124

Haidian

China's 'Silicon Valley' or **Zhongguancun**, is home to more than 400,000 of China's brightest scientists and teachers, and has become one of the nation's most important centres of science and technology research. For the lay

Right: the Beijing Aquarium.

Left: artist enclaves like 798 are making Beijing one of the hottest markets in the world for contemporary art.

100,000 seat **National Stadium** is dubbed the 'Bird's Nest' because of its steel-band exterior support, while the **National Aquatics Centre** has been nicknamed the 'Water Cube', and is sheathed in bubble-like transparent membranes.
SEE ALSO OLYMPICS, P.84–5

Art District

After the government booted out Beijing's bohemian artist community from the Old Summer Palace in the 1990s, they packed up their brushes and migrated to pockets in the east of the city. The most established of these is **Factory 798**, in Dashanzi, not far from the airport, where a grid of abandoned warehouses has been converted into galleries, studios and arty little wine bars. The area is site of the annual **Dangdai International Art Festival** or DIAF as it is better known. **The Liquor Factory** (Jiuchang) is a bit of a trek but is gaining some popularity, while **The Artists' Village** is tucked away in the dusty village of Songzhuang.
SEE ALSO MUSEUMS AND GALLERIES, P.77

You can get a good soak and wash off the Beijing grime in one of dozens of **hot spring resorts** such as **Jihua Spa** in the north of the city beyond the Sixth Ring Road in Chanping district. There are pools where fish nibble your toes, bubble baths, mud baths and medicinal soaks to soothe arthritic bones. Choose the resort wisely; the cheaper ones tend to be a bit grubby. *See also Pampering, p.95.*

person, though, the area is famous for its electronic super-malls, where you can buy everything from an iBook to an electronic dictionary.

Further north, out beyond the Fourth Ring Road, is the prestigious **Beijing University** (Beijing Daxue, or 'Beida' for short). The campus has park-like grounds with a quiet lake, and a classical Chinese pagoda with pavilions and stone figures. The students have been involved in most of the political upheavals of the 20th century, from the May the Fourth Movement of 1919 to the Tiananmen protests of 1989. In recent years, though, the students have become known for their conservative nationalism. The university area is well supplied with bars and cheap restaurants, with the main concentration around Wudaokou.

Around 2km (1 mile) to the east on the Third Ring Road, squeezed in among the new

buildings and the factories, is **Dazhongsi** ③ (Temple of the Great Bell), dating from AD743. On display are some 160 ancient bells, from tiny 150g specimens to the bronze giant that gives the temple its name.

Olympic Village

In its desire to dress to impress when it hosts the Olympic Games, China has built a mini Olympic city in a sprawling part-forested park just north of the Fourth Ring Road. The **China Olympic Village** ④ is a residential complex for athletes competing in the 2008 Games; it will be sold off as commercial flats afterwards. The village and many of the new sports venues have been built on the ancient north–south axis which divides the capital running up through the Forbidden City and the Bell and Drum Towers. Most of the main Olympic venues are just south of the Village. The

Western Fringes

The landscaped gardens and lavish palaces built outside Beijing for the pleasure of the emperor and his court are now open to anyone who wants to escape the urban sprawl. In the hills and valleys to the immediate west of the city are a number of tranquil temples and other sites of historical – and prehistorical – significance. If the weather is clear, they provide an ideal vantage point to survey the city from afar and offer excellent opportunities for hiking or simply a great place for a picnic. The hills are a blaze of red and yellow in autumn. Further north are the impressive imperial tombs of the Ming emperors.

The Summer Palaces

Northwest of the city, are two expansive sites where the Qing emperors built dozens of palaces, pavilions and temples in a contrived idyllic landscape of artificial hills, lakes and canals. The older complex, the **Old Summer Palace** ① (Yuanmingyuan), was largely destroyed by foreign troops at the end of the Second Opium War. The European Baroque ruins create an eerie atmosphere.

The **New Summer Palace** ② (Yiheyuan), built as a replacement by the Empress Dowager Cixi at the end of the 19th century, was also plundered by foreign troops, but most of the buildings survived or were restored. Highlights include Kunming Lake, which covers about two-thirds of the park, **Longevity Hill** (Wanshoushan), a string of ornate halls and pagodas, the **Long Corridor** (Changlang), a magnificent 728m- (2,388ft-) long covered walkway, and the famous **Marble Boat** (Qingyanfang).
SEE ALSO PALACES AND HOMES, P.90, 93

Fragrant Hills Park ③

Whether you're escaping Beijing's heat or just its crowds, a trip to **Fragrant Hills Park** (Xiangshan Gongyuan), only an hour's drive to the northwest, is a convenient day trip. The 550m (1,804ft) Fragrant Hill can be reached either on foot or by cable car.

There are a string of temples, including the Tibetan-

style **Temple of Clarity** (Zhaomiao), the spectacular **Biyunsi** (Temple of the Azure Clouds) and the remains of **Xiangshan Temple**. Near the eastern gate stands the I.M. Pei-designed, and beautifully situated, **Fragrant Hills Hotel**.

The **Fragrant Hills Botanical Gardens** (Xiangshan Zhiwuyuan) is a conservatory filled with lush tropical plants and plastic dinosaurs. Nearby is the **Wofosi** (Temple of the Reclining Buddha). The 5m (16ft) statue weighs 54 tonnes. SEE ALSO HOTELS, P.67; PARKS AND GARDENS, P.97–8; TEMPLES, CHURCHES AND MOSQUES, P.124–5

Western Temples

The **Tanzhesi** (Temple of the Poor and the Mulberry Tree), Beijing's oldest Buddhist temple, is on **Tanzheshan Hill**, about an hour away from the city by taxi. It is easy to com-

Left: boating around the New Summer Palace.

bine a visit here with a trip to the imposing **Jietaisi** (Ordination Terrace Temple). Both are delightful because of their rural setting and peaceful isolation, particularly on weekdays.
SEE ALSO TEMPLES, CHURCHES AND MOSQUES, P.125

Marco Polo Bridge

Marco Polo was said to have lavished great praise upon this structure some 700 years ago, hence the name. **The Marco Polo Bridge** ④ (Lugouqiao), 15km (9 miles) southwest of Beijing, was completely restored about 20 years ago but still bears patches of the original design. Some 501 lions line its ramparts, each slightly different from the other.

Peking Man

The site of the discovery of Peking Man, Sinanthropus pekinensis, lies close to the small town of **Zhoukoudian**, about 50km (31 miles) southwest of Beijing. Fossils and

Left: the Ming tombs.

human teeth had been discovered here for years, but in 1929 an almost complete skull was unearthed and caused an anthropological sensation. There is a small museum close to the **Peking Man Cave** (tel: 6930 1272; daily 8.30am–5pm; entrace fee; subway: taxi from Pinguoyuan), where a sort of eternal flame symbolises the importance of the hominoid's early use of fire.

The Ming Tombs

Thirteen of the 16 Ming emperors are buried in the **Ming Tombs** ⑤ (Shisanling, daily 8am–6pm; entrance fee) in a valley to the south of the Tianshou Mountains, 50km (31 miles) northwest of Beijing, although only three are open to the public — the **Tomb of Emperor Yongle** (Changling), the biggest and best preserved; the **Tomb of Emperor Wanli** (Dingling), in a subterranean palace; and the **Tomb of Zhaoling** (Longqing), who was buried along with three of his empresses. Each tomb is fronted by a statue-lined avenue and an arched memorial entrance gate.

After the Japanese invasion in 1937, archaeologists set about getting the **Peking Man** bones out of China. Packed in specially built wooden crates, they were handed on to the US Marine Corps for shipment to the US. However, it's unclear whether the skulls actually made it onto the ship – all that is known for sure is that they have never been seen since. Various theories have since surfaced. One has it that they were stolen by the Japanese and then lost in a shipwreck or buried in sites around Beijing by Chinese scientists.

The Great Wall

The Great Wall is the single greatest tourist attraction in China if not the world – it was voted one of its Seven Wonders after all. It looks as spectacular flanked by summer greenery as by winter snow, or by autumn yellows, oranges and browns. The construction visible today dates mostly from the 15th century and stretches for some 6,700km (4,163 miles). It is a structure of overwhelming physical presence; a vast wall of earth, brick and stone topped by an endless procession of stout towers. If it is more than a day's hiking you are after, a range of accommodation from cosy farmhouses to slick architecture installations sit within scrambling distance of the Wall.

Badaling

The most accessible section of the Wall – and consequently the most crowded – is at **Badaling** ①, 60km (37 miles) northwest of Beijing. Despite the hordes of sightseers, avoidable in the early mornings and in the colder months, Badaling has great scenery, restored forts and exhibitions.

The majority of visitors see Badaling as part of a tour, often taking in the Ming Tombs (see p.25) en route and sometimes also stopping at **Juyongguan Fortress**, built to guard the narrow, 20km- (12 mile-) long valley, and Beijing, against invading armies from the north.

Mutianyu

The Wall at **Mutianyu** ② is equally spectacular but less crowded than Badaling. A long section of restored Wall follows a high ridge, giving views over wooded ravines 90km (56 miles) northeast of Beijing. The nearest point on the Wall is a steep one-hour

Northern China's largest dam has created **Longqing Gorge**, often compared to Guilin's famous karst craggy land-scape, and makes a chilled side trip from Badaling. A giant sinuous escalator – disguised as a dragon – takes visitors to the top for sweeping views of the canyon, while tour boats bob in the water below. In the winter, its ice-sculpting and lantern festival is magical.

climb from the car park, though a cable car offers a breathtaking alternative and a luge-like slide is a quick way down. There are Western-style cottage restaurants and bed and breakfasts for those who want to stay overnight.

Left: take great care on steep, crumbling sections.

Left: visit in the early morning to avoid the crowds.

drops steeply into the valley to your right (south). There are farmhouse **hostels** and a boutique **ranch** along this section of the Wall.

The Hebei Coast

Ancient walls still enclose about half of the small market town and former garrison of **Shanhaiguan** ⑤, in Hebei Province, the place where the Wall meets the sea. The **East Gate**, rebuilt in 1639, is known as the **First Pass under Heaven**. Manchu troops rode through here to Beijing to replace the deposed Ming emperors in 1644.

As the Wall rises steeply inland, two sheer drops have to be climbed by ladder. From the top, you get a fantastic view of the Wall dropping below and then bounding over the plain towards the sea. In the opposite direction is the **Old Dragon's Head**, where bricks and earth crumble into golden sand at the edge of the Bohai Sea.

Simatai

Well established as a hiker's favourite, **Simatai** ③ shows the unrestored Great Wall at its most majestic, crowning a narrow ridge and sharp pinnacles. The site is 115km (71 miles) away from the city, and there is a popular 10km (6 miles) trek to **Jinshanling**, one of the few places where it is legal to camp overnight.

The scramble to **Viewing the Capital Tower** (Wangjing

Lou) demands a good head for heights, but rewards you with some of the best views and most exciting walking anywhere on the Wall. In places, you walk on sections just two bricks (40cm, 1.5in) wide, which locals call the *tianti*, or 'stairway to heaven'.

Huanghuacheng

Once one of the main garrison areas guarding the capital, **Huanghuacheng** ④, or Yellow Flower Wall, lies 60km (37 miles) north of Beijing, the closest the Wall gets to the city. It once had few tourist facilities, but in recent years has become an unfortunate example of rapid over-development. Climb up on either side from a small reservoir to the east of the road.

Several large towers along the ridge offer great views on both sides. A stone tablet lies on the floor of the largest tower. Further on, the Wall resembles a saw blade as it

Truly to experience the splendour of the Wall, you need to hike on it. Of old, parts of the Wall were used as routes for porters and itinerant traders. In this age of leisure-walking, many enthusiasts hope it will become the world's ultimate long-distance footpath. Since so much of the Wall is unrestored, seeing wilder sections need not be an endurance test. Walking is mostly on the Wall itself, so it is difficult to get lost, but the going is often slow. In some places, you may have no alternative but to leave and rejoin the Wall; in others, rickety piles of fallen bricks may be your only climbing aid. *See also Walks and Views, p.129.*

A–Z

In the following section Beijing's attractions and services are organised by theme, under alphabetical headings. All sights that lie within the atlas section at the end of the book are given a grid reference.

Architecture

Perhaps the most exciting aspect of a trip to Beijing is the opportunity to see an amazing range of architecture spanning thousands of years. There is the crumbling Great Wall, the blue-tiled Ming-dynasty prayer halls, Qing-dynasty palaces, 1950s Soviet-style beasts, and the extraordinary designs of modern architects that twist steel and glass into crazy projects in the sky. While Mao did his best to eradicate imperial China, enough remains to appreciate the beauty of the building of that time, and the present government appears to be making efforts to recreate some of what was destroyed.

Imperial Beijing

The finest examples of Ming-dynasty architecture are the prayer halls of the **Temple of Heaven**. Because of frequent wars and the fact that much was made in wood at the time, there is little to see that pre-dates this age.

Mao tore down most of the **old city wall** that was built during this time in the early 15th century. The wall, which follows the path of the city's Second Ring Road, is almost all gone except for a small stretch in the south near the Beijing Railway Station and a few of the old watchtowers including **Deshengmen** (next to Jishuitan subway), **Dongbianmen** in the southeast, **Zhengyangmen** in Qianmen and the **Old Observatory**.

The **Forbidden City** is the most extensive and best-preserved of Qing-dynasty workmanship. It was not meant to be a home for a mortal king but for the Son of

Heaven. According to legend, the Ming emperor Yongle, who began the building of the palace in 1409, received the plans from the hands of a Daoist priest who had descended from heaven especially for that purpose.

Left: Temple of Heaven.

SEE ALSO PALACES AND HOMES, P.86–9; MUSIC, DANCE AND THEATRE, P.78; TEMPLES, CHURCHES AND MOSQUES, P.118

Communist Beijing

The era of squat, grey Communist architecture has long gone, but if you want to be reminded of the brutal Soviet building style, head to Tiananmen Square *(see p.8–9)*. In the square itself is the **Monument to the People's Heroes** and the **Mao Mausoleum**. The square is also flanked by vast Soviet-style edifices. The **Great Hall of the People** on the west side is the largest of

Right: the Water Cube was designed by Australian and Chinese architects.

Left: imperial architecture at the Lama Temple.

more than 3,000 bubble-like pillows. The **National Stadium**, or 'Bird's Nest' is a Swiss-Chinese creation. This saddle-shaped lattice-work of steel will, of course, be open before the Olympics.

SEE ALSO MUSIC, DANCE AND THEATRE, P.78, 80; OLYMPICS, P.84–5

The Great Wall

The astonishing project took nearly 20 centuries to complete and involved millions of conscripted labourers.

The Ming-dynasty Ten Thousand Li Great Wall averages 8m (26ft) high and 7m (23ft) wide. Some sections are broad enough to allow five or six soldiers to ride side by side. Surveyors planned the route so that, where possible, the outer (generally north-facing) wall was higher. Countless parallel walls, fortified towers, beacon towers, moats, fortifications and garrisons completed a complex system. Local military units supervised construction. Elaborate wooden scaffolding, hoists and pulleys, and occasionally iron girders aided the builders. To speed up the construction process, prefabricated stone parts were used for beacon towers, including lintels, gate blocks and gullies.

SEE ALSO THE GREAT WALL, P.26–7

these behemoths. Directly opposite is the **National Museum of China**.

Modern Metropolis

The remit for modern developers simply seems to be to outdo each other in height, size or oddness – in some cases with little regard to the quality of materials or workmanship, or the safety of their workers.

The **National Grand Theatre** or the 'The Egg', on Chang'an Jie next to Tiananmen Square, opened in December 2007. Designed by French architect Paul Andreu, the shiny hemisphere of titanium and glass which looks a bit like an alien pod is semi-

Sadly, the restoration of much of the city's imperial buildings has been complicated by the dearth of workers skilled in such arts as *trompe l'œil* painting and paper-hanging. The craftsmen involved in the restoration all have decades of training and experience – but no successors to whom they can pass on skills.

transparent so the audience inside can see the sky.

Over in the Central Business District, where the towers get ever taller, is the **CCTV Building**, along the Third Ring Road, due to open before the Summer Olympics. Rem Koolhaas and Ole Scheeren designed the 230m- (755ft-) high zigzag doughnut (it is unclear how the elevators are going to work) with a smaller sister building shaped like a trapezoidal boot.

Two of the Olympic venues are also raising some architectural eyebrows. Up in the north in the Olympic Village, the **National Aquatics Centre**, or 'Water Cube', which opened in February 2008, is a glowing blue block made of

A good example of China's obsession with being the biggest is the **Great Observation Wheel** project in Chaoyang Park. Much like the London Eye, the 208m- (682ft-) high wheel, which will be the tallest in the world, will offer aerial vistas of the city. It is scheduled to start spinning in 2009.

Bars

As the numbers of expatriates have multiplied, so the city's bar scene has expanded to take in their multifarious thirsts. Beijing offers everything from the sophisticated cocktail lounge to the streetside RMB5 beer joints. There are bars with a view; bars underground; bars with a garden; and bars on a rooftop. There are Chinese-style karaoke bars; German microbreweries; French wine bars, Italian grappa joints and Japanese sake clubs. Some bar staff are dressed as French maids or policewomen, but there is usually no dress code for clientele except for a ban on flip-flops in upscale places. *See also Nightlife, p.82–3.*

Along Chang'an Jie

Writer's Bar
Raffles Beijing Hotel, 33 Dongchang'an Jie, Dongcheng; tel: 6526 3388 ext. 4181; daily noon–midnight; subway: Wangfujing; map p.136 B4
With piano music tinkling in the background, the elite sip scotch, smoke cigars and snack on caviar and oysters while reclining on the chesterfield sofa. Thus is Raffles' Writer's Bar.

The Lake District

No Name
3 Qianhai Dongyan (just south of Yinding Bridge), Houhai, Xicheng; tel: 6401 8541; daily noon–2am; subway: Gulou; map p.134 A3
The choice of a crackling fire in winter or the summer sunshine filtering in through the lakeside windows makes No Name the best bar by far around Houhai Lake. It was the first to open and, despite repeated threats to demolish the site, it might well outlast them all. Come and make friends with one of their three dusty white cats and enjoy a beer.

Gulou

Bed
17 Zhangwang Hutong, off Jiugulou Dajie, Xicheng; tel: 8400 1554; daily 6pm–2am; subway: Gulou; map p.134 A3
This cave-like courtyard bar mixes the city's best mojitos. Lounge around on opium beds or dance to the DJ in the middle courtyard.

Candyfloss Café
35 Dongmianhua Hutong (behind the Academy of Drama on Nanluogu Xiang), Dongcheng; tel: 6405 5775; daily 7pm–midnight; subway: Gulou; map p.134 B2
Beijing's most romantic bar has a tree-filled garden and individual living-room-styled cubby holes. Drinks are not amazing, but the ambience is.

Left: Suzie Wong's, *see p.83.*

If Bar
67 Beiluogu Xiang (directly north of Nanluogu Xiang), Dongcheng; tel: 6406 9496; daily 1pm–2am; subway: Gulou; map p.134 B3
Much use is made of glass floors, deep cream, blue lights and corkscrew and jigsaw designs. Music is chilled Massive Attack and DJ Krush, drinks are reasonably priced, and the vibe is definitely cool.

The Embassy District

Face
26 Dongcaoyuan, Gongti Nanlu, Chaoyang; tel: 6551 6788; www.facebars.com; daily noon–2am; subway: taxi from Chaoyangmen; map p.135 E1
Face is designer Asia chic. This converted schoolhouse has been made to look like a well-heeled expatriate's apartment filled with stone Buddha heads and Indonesian furniture. Beijing's branch follows equally exclusive spots in Shanghai, Bangkok and Jakarta.

Manzo
27 Liangmaqiao Road, Nuren Jie, Chaoyang; tel: 6436 1608; daily

Left: a connoisseur's collection.

Stone Boat Café

Ritan (near West Gate), Chaoyang; tel: 6501 9986; daily noon–late; subway: taxi from Chaoyangmen; map p.137 D4

This lovely bar in Ritan juts out over a lake fringed with sculpted rocks, willows and a pagoda. Come summertime, the bar hosts evening concerts of everything from drum'n'bass to Brazilian jazz.

The Tree

43 Sanlitun Beijie Youyi Youth Hostel, Chaoyang; tel: 6415 1954; daily 1pm–late; subway: Gongti Beilu; map p.135 E2

The favourite haunt of grizzly expat men, this place is worth a mention for its busy buzzing atmosphere until late, prize-winning crispy pizzas and bottled Belgian beer.

Central Business District

Centro

Kerry Centre Hotel, 1 Guanghua Lu, Chaoyang; tel: 6561 8833; 24 hours; subway: Guomao; map p.137 D4

Centro has outlasted many of its rivals with a winning blend of live jazz, a cavernous wine cellar and some good cocktail happy-hour deals. Not cheap but Centro is classy.

12SQM is Beijing's smallest bar. This little booze patch, exactly 12sq m of course, is on Nanluogu Xiang (map p.134 B2) and can, at a squeeze, fit 19 people, making it Beijing's cosiest. It has a good selection of Irish malts and for Sunday brunch does a mean Aussie steak pie.

6pm–midnight; subway: taxi from Maizidian Xilu

Fabulous sake and sochu bar opened by an official taster and thus a favourite of the Japanese expatriate.

Mingle

7 Sanlitun Beilu (northwest of 3.3), Chaoyang; tel: 6417 0090; daily 9pm–2am; subway: Gongti Beilu; map p.135 E3

Fans of loud hip hop and those with a fetish for uniforms will enjoy this new novelty bar. Girls dress as nurses, French maids, schoolgirls and police-women, while the men dress as schoolboys and policemen.

Pepper

Chaoyang Ximen (West Gate of Chaoyang Park), Chaoyang; tel: 6592 0988; daily 8pm–4am; subway: taxi from Liangmahe; map p.135 E3

A lively and less sleazy option to Suzie Wong's *(see p.83)* next door. The cocktail juggling shows are a riot. The cocktails are also mind-blowingly good, and inventively named – try their killer Adios Motherf*cker.

Q Bar

5/F Eastern Inn, Nansanlitun Lu, Chaoyang; tel: 6595 9239; daily 6pm–late; subway: taxi from Chaoyangmen; map p.135 E2

This chilled club-bar has a great ambience despite being tucked on the fifth floor of the dodgy-looking Eastern Inn. Service has sunk of late, but lighting is sexy, there's a summer deck, the sofas are sinkable and the cocktails are stellar.

Below: Sanlitun Bar Street.

As a measure of how far Beijing has come since Mao's day, 2007 saw the opening of the city's first – and hopefully last – branch of American chain **Hooters**. In their shiny tights, orange hot pants and low-cut, cleavage-enhanced vest tops, the Chinese staff entertain with renditions of *I'm a Little Teapot* and a dodgy version of the chicken dance. Despite the greasy food and overpriced beer, the brutally lit restaurant packs in a regular crowd of drunken expatriates and bemused locals.

33

Beijing Opera

One of the most conventionalised forms of theatre to be found anywhere in the world, Beijing Opera requires years of training to master. Actors often undergo seven years of gruelling schooling as children, after which they are selected for specific roles: male, female, warrior or clown. The emphasis is on Confucian morality: goodness is upheld and evil is punished. Performances combine ritualised movements with acrobatics, bold make-up, elaborate costumes, piercing singing and heart-stopping percussion. While Beijing Opera is undoubtedly an acquired taste, for a newcomer a performance is an unforgettable experience.

History

Although Chinese theatre in the form of skits, vaudeville, puppet shows and shadow plays has existed for over 1,000 years, formal music-drama has its origins in the 13th-century Yuan dynasty. This evolved into more than 300 different styles of Chinese Opera, but today the highly stylised Beijing *(jingju)* variety – dating from the 1800s – is by far the most popular.

In the old days, permanent theatres were a rarity, even in Beijing. As a result, opera was performed on the streets and in the marketplaces – a sign of its popularity with ordinary people. It was a useful way for them to learn about life outside the narrow circle of their own day-to-day existence.

Under Mao, traditional operas were banned and replaced by the eight model plays which expressed key Communist principles. After Mao's death in 1976, the genre was allowed to return to its roots.

The Legends

Many operas draw upon popular legends, folk or fairy tales, or classical literature; tales such as *The Three Kingdoms*, *The Dream of the Red Chamber* or *Journey to the West* are much better known in China than their equivalent literary classics in the West.

Beijing Opera is a composite of different expressive art

Above: female performers are a recent addition.

forms: literature, song, dialogue, mime and acrobatics (disciplines normally separated in Western theatre). Plots are based on historical stories or folklore with which audiences are already familiar. The main division is between *wenxi* (civilian plays) and *wuxi* (military dramas), but there are also comedies and skits. *Wenxi* pieces are more like Western drama, and describe daily life. The *wuxi*, on the other hand, consist mainly of fights, and tell of historical

The most celebrated Beijing Opera performer, **Mei Lanfang** (1894–1961) was a master of the *dan* role (a female role played by a man). Mei was born into a family of performers. He began studying opera as a child, making his stage debut at 11. By the time he was 20, he was already a household name. In 50 years as a *dan* performer, Mei played more than 100 female roles, including concubines, generals and goddesses. He was also an ambassador abroad, taking the ancient art form to Japan, Russia, India, Egypt and the US – where he made friends with actor Charlie Chaplin. Visit the **Mei Lanfang Memorial** to learn more about his life. *See also The Lake District, p.13.*

Left: a *jing*'s (warrior) presence dominates the stage.

tel: 6303 6830; subway: Qianmen; map p.136 A3
Opera only makes up a fraction of nightly shows here, which also include comedy skits, acrobatics and magic, but it's a lively place, and snacks and tea are provided.

Liyuan Theatre
Qianmen Jianguo Hotel, 175 Yongan Lu, Xuanwu; tel: 6301 6688; subway: Hepingmen; map p.139 E2
What it lacks in history, Liyuan makes up for in getting the audience involved. Guests can watch performers put on their make-up and even try on costumes and make-up themselves.

Zhengyici Beijing Opera Theatre
220 Xiheyan Dajie, Xuanwu; tel: 8315 1649; subway: Hepingmen; map p.136 A3
Perhaps the best place to see Beijing Opera. This beautifully renovated ancient wooden theatre puts on nightly performances of opera excerpts.

> For a sampling of Beijing Opera visit the Palace of Prince Gong *(see p.90)* on Lake Houhai. It contains Beijing's only preserved Qing-dynasty theatre.

wars and battles, making great use of acrobatics.

The Cast

Before the 1930s, all the roles were required to be played by men. There are four main character types: *sheng*, scholars or nobleman; *chou*, clowns; *jing*, warriors; and *dan*, female roles. Mastery of singing, of course, is essential, while clowns are also often required to demonstrate acrobatic prowess. All actors must hone the fine body movements that are the opera's style. An actor's training includes learning how to apply the elaborate make-up that serves to identify each character.

Theatres

Chang'an Grand Theatre
7 Jianguomennei Dajie, Dongcheng; tel: 6510 1309; www.changantheater.com; subway: Jianguomen; map p.136 D4
This massive glass-fronted theatre next to the Beijing International Hotel is pricey but puts on quality performances and subtitles shows.

Huguang Guildhall
3 Hufang Qiao, Xuanwu; tel: 6351 8284; www.beijing huguang.com; subway: Hepingmen; map p.139 E2
With a history of over 200 years, this old theatre is one of the most atmospheric places to see traditional opera.

Lao She Teahouse
3 Qianmen Xidajie, Xuanwu;

> If you don't have time to take in a performance at the theatre, just switch on your hotel's television. National channel CCTV11 broadcasts all kinds of Chinese Opera all day.

Below: a traditional *dan* character.

Cafés

Tea is the traditional drink of choice for the Chinese, but a newly affluent middle class is fuelling the capital's thirst for good cafés. Seattle-based coffee chain Starbucks probably serves the best-value caffeine per cup, but there is a growing crop of individually run cafés that serve a decent brew of imported beans, luring customers with free wireless, magazines and decadent desserts. Several photographers and artists have opened little coffee nooks in Nanluogu Xiang, creating a space to display, and hopefully to flog, their work. For a traditional tea experience see *Teahouses, p.116–17*.

Lake District

Coffeesalon.com
1 Yandai Xiejie (entrance of Yinding Hutong), Houhai, Dongcheng; tel: 8402 6544; daily 10am–10pm; subway: Gulou; map p.133 E3
Cramped it may be, but Coffeesalon.com has the best cup in town. Beans are imported raw and roasted in the shop. Free wireless.

Gulou

Alba
79 Nanluogu Xiang, Dongcheng; tel: 6407 3730; daily noon–2am; subway: Gulou; map p.134 B2
This quirky little café may not have the most comfortable seating, but it does have the best home-made ginger beer – think strong and tangy – and a wicked chocolate mousse. Wireless is available.

Arts Coffee Haven
25 Guozijian Jie, Dongcheng; tel: 6405 2047; daily 9am–11pm; subway: Andingmen; map p.134 B3
In a beautiful location just down from the Confucius Temple *(see p.120–1)*, this unusual café has coddled cats, Hindu-inspired Buddhist wall murals – they sell lassis and Indian jewellery – red lanterns and rosewood furniture. Look for the octagonal window. Wireless is available.

Mistica
Zhangzizhong Road, Dongcheng; tel: 6403 0688; daily 9am–9pm; subway: Zhangzizhonglu; map p.134 B2
This Argentinian café's big draw is its location in the dilapidated former campus for the Academy of Social Sciences, a beautiful crumbling French colonial-style mansion. Comparatively cheap drinks and tango classes at night.

Sandglass
1 Mao'er Hutong Nanluogu Xiang, Dongcheng; tel: 6402 3529; daily noon–2am; subway: Gulou; map p.134 B2
This Mongolian-owned dive is squashed into a tiny courtyard house and is perennially popular with locals. Rather than their average coffee, relax with a glass of wine and enjoy the ethnic Mongolian music.

The 32cafe
32 Qianliang Hutong, Dongcheng; tel: 6401 7697; daily 11am–11pm; subway: Dongsi; map p.134 B2
This hutong café has its own bathroom, stacks of books, a little garden, high ceilings, massive windows and a craft shop. Next door is the French-inspired **Caribou Café**.

Vineyard Café
39 Wudaoying Hutong, Dongcheng; tel: 6402 7961; www.vineyardcafe.cn; Tue–Sun 11.30am–10.30; subway: Yonghegong; map p.134 B3
The British-run Vineyard has everything – coffee, wireless, hearty English breakfasts, a pub-parlour front room, an outdoor courtyard section and a lounge sofa area. They play funky music, hold movie nights, and best of all, they have their own bathroom (rare for hutong venues).

Waiting for Godot
Building 4, 24 Jiaodaokou Dongdajie, Dongcheng; tel: 6407 3093; daily 10.30am–midnight; subway: Beixinqiao; map p.134 B3
While Waiting for Godot caters to the moody, arty type it escapes pretentiousness. The walls are painted black and pasted with pensive posters of Samuel Becket and Björk, and tables have 1920s green reading

Left and Below: At Café.

8am–8pm; subway: Gongti Beilu; map p.135 E3
This is one of the best places for coffee and a fry-up hangover cure; the Portuguese-Peruvian owners are very friendly. Wireless is available.

The North

At Café
4 Jiuxianqiao Lu, Dashanzi, Chaoyang; tel: 6438 7264; daily 10am–midnight; subway: taxi from Liangmahe
At Café is a cute brick cubby hole with a loft and the place for artists and their admirers to snack on pasta, creamy desserts and coffee.

Jackie Chan Café
The Gate Building L107, 19 Zhongguancun Nandajie, Haidian; subway: taxi from Wudaokou
This Starbucks-esque coffee house was opened by the eponymous kung fu legend. The décor is all Chan, and TVs screen his movies.

Western Fringes

Sculpting in Time
50 Maimai Jie, Xiangshan (Fragrant Hills), Haidian; tel: 8259 8296; daily 9.30am–11.30pm; subway: taxi from Wudaokou
This relaxed student-style dive is hit-and-miss, but has good coffee and free wireless.

The furore over the Forbidden City Starbucks was a battle which pitted a Chinese public whipped into a xenophobic over-reaction by the media against an American coffee-house chain accused of cultural insensitivity. In the summer of 2007, Starbucks eventually caved in to public pressure and closed its branch in the ancient palace after seven years on the site. The Chinese public claimed Starbucks's Forbidden City venue undermined the integrity of their imperial culture. The irony is that throughout the historic site, vendors continue to purvey all kinds of culture-insulting tack, and Western drinks including Budweiser beer.

lamps. There's wireless, the coffee is great, but don't come here for the food.

Xiao Xin
103 Nanluogu Xiang, Dongcheng; tel: 6403 6956; daily 9.30am–midnight; subway: Gulou; map p.134 B3
This popular café is crammed with all kinds of junk – an old radio, piles of tattered magazines – but what draws the

old faithful to its mustiness are its home-baked cheese-cakes. Wireless is available.

The Embassy District

Bookworm
4 Nansanlitun Lu, Chaoyang; tel: 6586 9507; www.beijing bookworm.com; daily 9am–1am; subway: Gongti Beilu; map p.135 E2
Now a Beijing institution, the Bookworm operates as a library (16,000 volumes), a bookshop and a venue for author talks and writing workshops. Beware the pretentious types posing with their laptops. The menu is overpriced and lacklustre, but it is a good place to settle down with a book and a drink.

Café de Niro
1/F, Tongli Studios, Sanlitun Beijie, Chaoyang; tel: 6416 9400; daily 10am–midnight; subway: Gongti Beilu; map p.135 E2
More style than substance, this sleek white café has wireless, friendly staff and half-price desserts after 9pm.

Sparrow's Café
103, 30 Sanlitun Beilu, Chaoyang; tel: 6413 0345; daily

Children

T he nation's love of children is nowhere more evident than in the warmth the Chinese show to infant tourists, especially if those infant tourists are blond and blue-eyed. And while the main attractions of Beijing – imperial palaces, ancient ruins and long meals of foreign-tasting foods – are not especially child-friendly, the city has plenty to delight toddlers and teenagers, from acrobatic shows to kite-flying to shopping for cheap designer fashions. And as more expatriate workers bring their families to live in Beijing, dozens of businesses and services have sprung up to cater to the needs of youngsters.

Beijing Aquarium

Gaoliangqiao Xiejie, Haidian; tel: 6217 6655 ext. 9; www.bj-sea.com; daily 9am–5pm; entrance charge (children under 1.2m/4ft free); subway: Xizhimen; map p.132 B3

Freshly stocked and modern, the aquarium does a better job at looking after its animals than the wretched zoo next door. There are shows with performing seals and dolphins, and a giant reef undulating with sharks and manta rays. The **Blue Zoo** (Gongren Tiyuchang Nanlu, Worker's Stadium South Gate, Chaoyang; tel: 6591 3397; entrance fee; daily winter: 8.30am–6.30pm, summer: 8am–8pm; subway: Chaoyangmen; map p.135 D2) is a smaller aquarium.

China Puppet Theatre

1 Anhua Xili, Beisanhuan, Chaoyang; tel: 6425 4798; www.puppetchina.com; subway: taxi from Andingmen

Bringing culture to the kids: puppet shows here are full-on affairs and cover everything from Chinese classics to western fairy tales to Olympics-inspired theatre. Performances are on weekend evenings only.

Fundazzle

Gongti Nanmen, Chaoyang; tel: 6506 9066; Mon–Fri 9am–5.30pm, Sat–Sun 9am–7.30pm; children entrance fee, Mon–Fri adults free; subway: Chaoyangmen; map p.135 E1

Left: the Blue Zoo.

A giant indoor play-gym with tunnels, slides, trampolines and toy houses. At weekends, Fundazzle hold shows and kids' craft classes.

Happy Valley Amusement Park

Wuji Beilu, Dongsihuan, Chaoyang; tel: 6738 9898; www.happyvalley.com.cn; Mon–Fri hours vary; subway: taxi from Sihui

This massive funfair opened in 2006 and has had rave reviews. Kids love the Ant Kingdom and the roller coasters. A step down from Happy Valley is **Beijing Amusement Park**, across from Longtang Park and the Disney rip-off,

Thriving on the advertising, Beijing's English-language expatriate magazines all have children's pull-out sections with listings, events and features. *City Weekend* devotes three or four pages to juniors each issue. *That's Beijing* has spawned a complete monthly called *tbjkids* (www.tbjkids.com).

Other fun child-friendly museums in the city are **Beijing Museum of Natural History** *(see p.76)*, which has animatronic dinosaurs, **Beijing Planetarium** *(see p.77)*, offering space rides in its digital universe theatre, and the **Beijing Science and Technology Museum** *(see p.77)*, which has robots.

Left: a little empress explores Ditan Park.

6433 3960/6433 2345 (emergencies); www.unitedfamily hospitals.com; daily 8.30am–5.30pm, emergencies 24hr; subway: taxi from Liangmahe

English-speaking, international-standard medical services; note consultations are not cheap. Expect to pay around US$100 to see a doctor. It is the hospital of choice for pregnant expatriates with good insurance packages.

NAPPIES
Leyou
111 Jiaodaokou Nandajie, Dongcheng; tel: 6405 6406; daily 9am–8pm; subway: Beixinqiao; map p.134 B3
China's answer to Mothercare. This chain of baby stores is easily spotted by its yellow sign. Stocks nappies, baby food and bibs.

TOYS
Shengtangxuan
38 Guizojian Jie, Dongcheng; tel: 8404 7179; daily 9am–7pm; subway: Andingmen; map p.134 B3
Beijing's only handmade traditional toy shop. The nonagenarian native of Manchuria has been making toys for over 80 years. Look out for his magic moppets, misshapen clay animals, spinning tops, and cloth lions and tigers.

Sony Explorascience
Chaoyang Park, Chaoyang; tel: 6501 8800; www.explora science.com.cn; Mon–Fri 9.30am–6pm, Sat–Sun 9.30am–7.30pm; subway: taxi from Gongtibeilu
This flash centre offers a hands-on and fun way for children to learn about science, nature and technology.

Shijingshan Amusement Park (go to Bajiao Youleyuan on subway line one).

Parks
The parks and lakes can be a lot of fun for young ones. You can hire bird- or battleship-shaped boats at **Houhai**, go magnetic fishing in **Ditan Park** and ride the merry-go-round in **Ritan**. The **Summer Palaces** are also great places for children, with plenty of space to run around – the Old Summer Palace has a maze – take boat trips on the lakes and chill out on the grass for a picnic.
SEE ALSO PALACES AND HOMES, P.90–3; PARKS AND GARDENS, P.97, 99

Shopping for Baby
BOOKS
Poplar Kids Republic Bookstore
1362, Building 13, Jianwai Soho, Guomao, Chaoyang; tel: 5869 3032; www.poplar.com.cn; daily 10am–7pm; subway: Guomao; map p.137 E4
Thousands of English and Chinese storybooks set in an innovative rainbow-painted play area. There are reading tubes, a magic carpet, and book talks and activities.

MEDICAL
Beijing United Family Hospital and Clinics
2 Jiangtai Lu, Lido, Chaoyang; tel:

Childproof Dining
Chinese restaurants are noisy, rambunctious affairs, and children will be made welcome in almost every establishment; kids will love getting their hands dirty making their own Beijing duck wraps. There is a sprinkling, however, that are especially child-friendly. Try **Din Tai Fung** *(see p.107)* on Xinyuan Xili, the fancy Taiwanese chain with a playroom, while **Dongbei Ren** *(see p.106)* is a fabulous North Chinese dumpling house which is a kaleidoscope of colour and a riot of singing staff. If your kid's a fussy eater then keep an eye out for one of the Western chain food favourites, including **Papa John's**, **TGI Friday's** and **Pizza Hut**. For ice cream indulge at **Gustomenta** on Sanlitun Beilu (map p.135 E3), with scoops of fresh *gelato*.

Chinese Medicine

The Chinese have been practising traditional medicine for around 5,000 years. Despite the popularity of Western treatments, the practice is thriving: Beijing has several university-affiliated research centres and hospitals devoted to Traditional Chinese Medicine (TCM). Typical TCM therapies include herbal medicines, acupuncture, *ba guan* (cupping), *gua sha* (scraping) and *qigong* exercises. While TCM is a long-term therapy, a visit to a herbalist with its jars of pungent powders is certainly fascinating. With the growing popularity of TCM in the west, Beijing's clinics offer a taster which can be continued back home.

Theory

The ideas behind traditional Chinese medicine, or TCM, are derived from the Daoist philosophy and date back more than 5,000 years. Two of the key concepts are that the body has an innate ability to heal its own illnesses – TCM doctors just prod it in the right direction for it to cure itself – and disease is caused by an imbalance of either *yin* (female life force) or *yang* (male life force).

Much hinges on a concept of the body having an essential energy, called *qi*. This *qi* flows around the body along 12 major paths or meridians, each associated with an organ. If one of the paths gets blocked, say by a sprain or an infection in one of the organs, illness results. Curiously, to date, Western scientists have been unable to link these paths with the nervous system or muscle groups.

Westerners are often drawn to TCM because it is generally accepted to be less invasive than Western medicine and has far fewer side effects. Many are also attracted by its main principle – which is healing the whole body rather than attacking the cause of the illness. TCM therapies, though, work in a gradual way, and treatments need to be taken regularly and over a long period of time before the benefits are fully felt.

TCM Consultation

A consultation with a TCM doctor is a little different from one with your GP. First the doctor will ask you lots of questions about the ailment and also about your life –

> In Chinese medicine a body's *yin* and *yang* need to be in balance to be healthy. The two are opposites: *yin* represents water, cold, quiet and night; while *yang* represents fire, noise, dry and day. Restoring the balance is the crux of TCM's philosophy. Five key organs, the heart, lungs, kidneys, liver and spleen, known collectively as the *Zang*, are responsible for controlling the main *yin-yang* balance in the body.

stress, what kind of food you've been eating, sleep patterns and dreams. The most highly trained doctors will then take your pulse at 12 different points – corresponding to the 12 *qi* paths. Western measuring techniques have identified subtle difference in these 12 pulses. Finally, because the tongue is considered a good indicator of a person's health, the doctor will examine your tongue, paying particular attention to its colour and texture. Like the sole of a foot, the tongue can be divided into regions which relate to parts of the body.

Acupuncture

The needles in acupuncture stimulate points along the *qi* path or paths that the TCM doctor decides are blocked, thus causing the pain or illness. The needles are thought to restore the normal flow of *qi*, thus assisting the body in healing itself. Acupuncture has had particular success in helping women using IVF to conceive. The treatment is more

Left: a dramatic example of traditional cupping.

quite uncomfortable. Like acupuncture, it helps to restore the flow of *qi*. It is often used to treat colds and fevers.

In *gua sha* (scraping) the skin is oiled down and then scraped repeatedly with a hard but smooth object, say a ceramic spoon, buffalo horn or metal cup. The procedure breaks capillaries near the surface, causing red speckling. It is most often used to treat fever and digestive problems.

TCM Clinics

Beijing Massage Hospital
7 Baochan Hutong, Xinjiekou, Xicheng; tel: 6616 1064; daily 8–11.45am, 1.30–10pm; subway: Jishuitan; map p.133 D2
Offers consultations and many of the TCM therapies including massage, *ba guan*, *gua sha* and acupuncture. Over half of the masseurs are blind. Also teaches courses in Chinese medicine practice.

Comfortable Blind Massage
18 Zhongfan Li, Nansanlitun Lu, Chaoyang; tel: 6507 0036; daily 9.30am–11pm; subway: Gongti Beilu (after July 2008); map p.135 E2
Inexpensive blind massages as well as *ba guan* and *gua sha*. For the price of a return taxi a masseur will come to your hotel room.

Ping Xin Tang Clinic
4/F, 218-2 Wangfujing Dajie, Dongcheng; tel: 6523 5566; subway: Wangfujing; map p.136 B4
The doctors here – some speak English – are highly regarded. They offer treatment for a wide range of illnesses, including serious ailments. Registration fee is around RMB150.

uncomfortable than painful; the secret is to relax. Moxibustion, the burning of herbs at the puncture point, is sometimes used in conjunction with acupuncture.

TCM Medicines

Some 70 percent of TCM medicines are made of plant matter, including flowers, herbs, roots and tree bark. The rest is made up of animal parts and minerals. Many Beijing pharmacies also have a herbalist who will mix up a prescription and wrap it in paper, often into individual one-dose packages. Larger pharmacies will boil up the medicine into a tea to take away. Usually it is very bitter and does not smell too good, either.

Ba Guan and *Gua Sha*

In *ba guan* (cupping), light-bulb-shaped glass suction cups are placed along the back, either side of the spine, pulling up the skin and leaving dark purple bruises that last for about a week. The procedure can be

Below: reflexology and lizard elixir.

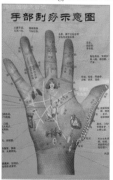

Environment

Beijing is one of the world's most exciting and fast-changing cities, but the price of this rapid development is choking pollution. The frequent smog not only casts the sky in dull leaden grey, but can also be a serious hazard to health. Spring sandstorms turn the heavens a beautiful pink and orange but clog the lungs with dust and leave a film of grime over parked cars and trees. While a booming economy has given locals the freedom for the first time to own private cars in large numbers, at rush hour Beijing's roads now compete with the world's most congested for frustration levels.

Pollution

The Olympics have forced Beijing's hand to take action about its hazardous levels of air pollution. Athletes are panicking about whether they can survive the smog, with British and American teams likely to carry specially designed air-pollution face masks this summer. Various pollution-alleviating measures have been implemented, to dubious results. It has relocated some polluting factories away from the city, periodically introduced a one-day ban on odd- then even-numbered licence plates to cut the number of private cars on the roads, and instigated a slow-down on some construction projects inside the city. While officially the number of 'blue sky' days, a simplified way of grading pollution, has increased, observers mock data, since the government has just moved monitoring stations from polluted areas inside the city to the suburbs where the air has always been cleaner. Whether their 'Olympic' measures are having any effect is neither here nor there for long-term Beijing residents. Once the Games are over, it will likely be back to business as usual, with construction returning to fever pitch and shuttered factories reopening.

A UN report in October 2007 found the average level of small particulate matter (called PM10) in the capital was eight times higher than recommended limits, and levels of poisonous gases such as sulphur dioxide, nitrogen dioxide and carbon monoxide have been on the rise since 2006. The problem is a mixture of Beijing's geography – the city lies in a shallow surrounded by mountains which trap airborne pollutants – the rising number of cars on the roads – roughly 1,000 new cars are added a day – the breakneck speed of construction in the city itself and the proximity of polluting factories and dirty coal-fired power stations nearby. The effects of air pollution are wide-ranging, from bronchitis to lung cancer. The World Health Organisation estimates around 400,000 people in China die every year from the effects of air pollution.

Even so, short-term visitors should not be too worried about the city's pollution. Take it easy when walking outside, and if the air quality is particularly bad, you are advised to stay indoors. Fortunately, conditions only get this serious a few days a year.

Sandstorms

As if the pollution were not enough to contend with, during the months of March and April, Beijing is also blighted by blistering sandstorms. The desertification of neighbouring regions, such as Inner Mongolia, through the misuse of land has brought the Gobi Desert so close to Beijing that there

Right: during rush hour the streets of Beijing come to a standstill, a key problem for tourists and residents alike.

Left: pollution is a grave concern for Olympic athletes.

sive pushiness, and that is putting it mildly. 'Terror has characterised every single one of my behind-the-wheel experiences,' wrote American journalist Ann Mah about driving in Beijing. Not all drivers are that bad, but visitors should take extra care on the roads and bear in mind that road signs are often ignored.

CONGESTION

The city's infrastructure has not kept pace with the capital's craze over new car ownership. The main ring roads and arteries sludge to a snail pace during rush hour – between 7am and 9am and 5pm and 7pm – and whenever it rains (everyone jumps into taxis). Avoid the Third Ring Road at all hours, though. While not yet as bad as London, the congestion here will inevitably get worse. You would be wise to avoid travelling at rush hour and take the subway if you can. The underground train network is cheap, fast and convenient, and by using it you will limit the polluting effect you would have had by taking a cab.

Consider 'offsetting' the CO_2 from your journey to and around Beijing through an organisation like **Climate Care** (www.climatecare.org). Its online calculator will tell you your carbon emissions for your trip and how much you should donate to the scheme.

---

are dunes 15km (9 miles) outside the Fifth Ring Road. Some years, fierce spring winds whip sand into the capital, causing the sky to turn fabulous colours, but dumping tonnes of dust into your mouth and eyes if you are outside, and coating everything in its path with a thick layer of sand. The average number of these sandstorms is around five a year.

Traffic
DRIVING STANDARDS

Chinese driving tests are not the most stringent, with the result that some of Beijing's drivers have rather alarming habits such as running red lights, reckless lane-changing to overtake, speeding, and zipping the wrong way down narrow one-way streets. Their road-handling style is marked by impatience and aggres-

---

To check Beijing's pollution: Pyongyang Square maintains a good blog on the city's air quality (www.pyongyang square.com/beijingair). The State Environmental Protection Agency publishes daily Air Pollution Indices in English (http://english.sepa.gov.cn). Anything under 100 is considered good; over 100 and you are advised to stay indoors if you have health problems; while you should probably leave Beijing if it tops 300.

Essentials

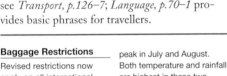

Beijing is single-mindedly transforming itself into an international city, and is driven by a desire to present its best face for the Olympics. This means that top-level hotels, shops and services are up to Western standards, although outside of these premier establishments not much English is spoken. The city is easy and cheap to navigate by taxi, tourist services are generally friendly, crime is low, and the Internet is everywhere, though restricted. For specific practical information on getting around Beijing see *Transport, p.126–7*; *Language, p.70–1* provides basic phrases for travellers.

Baggage Restrictions

Revised restrictions now apply on all international flights into and out of Beijing to the way in which liquids, gels and aerosols can be carried onto a plane. They must be in containers no bigger than 100ml and placed in a single (maximum one per passenger) transparent resealable bag, with a maximum capacity of one litre. Bags are available in the airport.

Climate

Beijing has a continental climate, with four clearly defined seasons.
Winter: lasts from November until April and is cold and dry with occasional snow. It is usually sunny. Temperatures sink to as low as -10°C (15°F) at night.
Spring: begins in April and is the shortest season. It is warm, dry and windy. In early spring, sandstorms blow in from the west and northwest. Average daytime temperature is around 20°C (70°F).
Summer: begins around the end of May and reaches its peak in July and August. Both temperature and rainfall are highest in these two months. It is often muggy; temperatures climb to over 30°C (85°F)and occasionally 35°C (95°F) or more.
Autumn: the sky is blue most of the time, and the air is cleaner, making it the best season to visit Beijing. Autumn is short, starting around the end of September, and is over by December. Average daytime temperature is around 20°C (70°F).

Customs

Expensive jewellery, equipment and the amount of foreign exchange should all be declared, and all imported items must be taken out again. Items that are imported and not taken out of the country again are subject to customs payments. Many books, newspaper reports, magazines and videos that are legal in the West may be deemed illegal in China, especially political or pornographic works.

Export restrictions apply to antiques. Antiques that can be exported carry a special customs sticker, which normally has a Temple of Heaven symbol. It is advisable to keep receipts for items bought, in case of spot checks.

Electricity

The standard for electricity in Beijing is 220 volts AC. Sockets are either two-pin flat blade or three-pin oblique flat blade. Occasionally you can find the three-pin rectangular-blade socket used in the UK. Hotels usually have a 110-volt or 120-volt outlet for shavers.

Embassies

Australia
21 Dongzhimenwai Dajie, Chaoyang; tel: 5140 4111; www.china.embassy.gov.au; subway: Dongzhimen; map p.135 E3
Canada
19 Dongzhimenwai Dajie, Chaoyang; tel: 6532 3536; www.beijing.gc.ca; subway: Dongzhimen; map p.135 E3
Ireland
3 Ritan Donglu, Chaoyang; tel: 6532 2691; www.embassyof

quate travel and health insurance before arriving in Beijing to cover medical emergencies, hospitalisation and all other possible medical expenses.

Beijing now has one international-standard hospital and a number of Western-run health clinics which are expensive but offer the peace of mind of Western-trained and English-speaking medical staff.

China-Japan Friendship Hospital

Yinghua Dongjie, Hepingli; Chaoyang; tel: 6422 3209; www.zryhyy.com.cn; subway: taxi from Hepingxiqiao

This Chinese-run hospital has a foreigners' wing, but not all doctors speak great English. Cheaper than overseas-run hospitals and clinics. Takes credit cards.

Beijing United Family Health Hospital and Clinics

2 Jiangtai Lu (close to Lido Hotel), Chaoyang; tel: 6433 3960, emergency: 6433 2345; www.unitedfamilyhospitals.com; subway: taxi from Sanyuanqiao

ireland.cn; subway: taxi from Chaoyangmen; map p.137 D4

New Zealand

1 Dong'er Jie, Ritan Lu, Chaoyang; tel: 6532 2731; www.nzembassy.com/china; subway: taxi from Chaoyangmen; map p.137 D4

United Kingdom

11 Guanghua Lu, Chaoyang; tel: 5192 4000; www.uk.cn; subway: taxi from Guomao; map p.137 D4

United States

3 Xiushui Beijie (southwest corner of Ritan Park), Chaoyang; tel: 6532 3831; http://beijing.usembassy-china.org.cn; subway: Jianguomen; map p.137 D4

Emergencies and Police

The Public Security Bureau or police wear dark blue-black uniforms and flat-top peaked hats. Few can speak English.

NUMBERS

Police: 110
Ambulance: 120
Fire: 119

Authorities promise that by the time of the Olympics,

emergency service numbers will have English-language answering staff.

Health and Medical Care

No vaccinations are required for China. It may be advisable to strengthen the body's resistance to hepatitis A infection by having a gammaglobulin injection before travelling.

MEDICAL SERVICES AND HOSPITALS

All visitors are strongly advised to take out ade-

Right: the devil is in the detail.

Squatting Toilet

Sitting Toilet

Expensive but Beijing's only international-standard hospital. Staff speak excellent English.

Beijing International SOS Clinic

Building C, BITIC Jingyi Building, Sanlitun Xi 5 jie, Chaoyang; tel: 6462 9112, emergency: 6462 9100; www.international sos.com; subway: taxi from Dongzhimen; map p.135 E3 English-speaking mainly Western doctors.

PHARMACIES

Pharmacies in China are of two kinds, those that sell predominantly Chinese medicine and those that sell predominantly Western medicine. Pharmacists in both kinds will offer advice and suggest medicine, although they may not speak English. Pharmacies keep varying hours, with many open until late at night.

The Wangfujing Drug Store

267 Wangfujing, Dongcheng; tel: 6525 2322; daily 8.30am–9.30pm; subway: Wangfujing; map p.136 B4

Internet

Beijing is a wired city. Most hotel rooms have free wireless and admittedly expensive business centres with computers. Western-style cafés including Starbucks also offer free wireless, and there are cheap Internet cafés *(wangba)* all over town. For as little as RMB10 an

hour you can surf with a room full of chain-smoking online game-addicted teenagers.

Media

China Daily is a state English-language newspaper. It includes listings of cultural events in Beijing, international news and good sports coverage. Several foreign daily papers can be bought in Beijing (a day late) from the big hotels, including Hong Kong's *South China Morning Post*, the *International Herald Tribune* and the *Financial Times*. Magazines available include *Newsweek*, *Time* and *The Economist*.

For local listings, free copies of English-language entertainment magazines can be picked up in Western-style restaurants and bars and are occasionally distributed in hotels. *That's Beijing* has the most comprehensive listings, while the twice-monthly *City Weekend* has a good pull-out map of Beijing. Both have listings in Chinese characters, which can be useful to show a taxi driver.

The only English-language domestic TV channel is the rather awful CCTV9.

Money

The Chinese currency is called renminbi (RMB; literally, 'people's money'). The basic unit is the yuan, often called kuai. One yuan is

worth 10 jiao, also called mao. Banknotes come in 100, 50, 20, 10, 5 and 1 yuan denominations; plus 5, 2 and 1 jiao.

Foreign currency and travellers' cheques can be changed in most hotels, and at branches of the Bank of China. For the latest rates see www.xe.com. Most ATM machines accept foreign cards connected to the Cirrus, Plus, AmEx, Visa and MasterCard networks. Credit cards are readily accepted in upscale establishments.

To change excess RMB back into foreign currency you must show your original exchange receipt. You are only allowed to change back a maximum of 50 percent of the original sum.

TIPPING

There is no culture of tipping, but waiters in large hotels and restaurants, as well as a few taxi drivers, do court tips.

Post

You will find postal facilities in most hotels. Letters and postcards to and from China take around a week. Parcels must be packed and sealed at the post office, to allow customs inspection. The main International Post Office is just north of Jianguomen intersection along the Second Ring Road (tel: 6512 8114; daily 8am–6.30pm; map p.137 D4).

Beijing time, which applies across China, is GMT +8 hours (EST +13 hours). There is no daylight savings time, so from early April to late October, Beijing is 7 hours ahead of London and 12 hours ahead of New York.

Note that the Internet is heavily censored in China. The BBC, Wikipedia and many free blog hosts are largely unavailable. But most popular email accounts are accessible, including gmail, hotmail and yahoo!

Telephones

You can make calls using public payphones, which can be found on most streets. To use them you need buy a prepaid 'IC' card from street-side newspaper kiosks and small shops. If you want to dial IDD you can buy prepaid Internet phonecards called 'IP' cards, which offer rates considerably lower than standard costs and can in theory be used from any phone – before dialling the number you wish to reach, you need to dial a local number printed on the card followed by a PIN number. Never pay the face value. A card worth RMB100 typically sells for around RMB35–40.

If you have a GSM mobile then you can probably use it in Beijing. Note Beijing has two mobile companies – China Mobile and China Unicom. China Mobile usually has better coverage.

DIALLING

The international code for China is 86. The area code for Beijing is 10, which does not need to be dialled for calls within the city, and is not included in the listed phone numbers in this guidebook.

Dial 115 for operator assistance with long-distance calls, and 114 for directory enquiries.

Tourist Information

Beijing's tourist information offices are not especially helpful, and mainly exist to sell tours. Most hotels offer guided tours to sights inside and outside Beijing. Larger hotels organise their own tours; others arrange trips through CITS or smaller travel companies.

China International Travel Service Beijing (CITS)
28 Jianguomenwai, Chaoyang; tel: 6515 7671; www.cits. com.cn; subway: Jianguomen; map p.137 D4
This state-run service has offices in several hotels and at some tourist venues.

TRAVEL AGENTS
China eTours
2001 Guangqumen Nanxiaojie, Chongwenmen; tel: 6716 0201 ext. 1010; www.etours.cn; subway: Chongwenmen; map p.137 D2
Takes bookings over the Internet and the phone.

CnAdventure
5th Floor, Daxiang Investment Building, A1 Dongbinhe Lu, Dongcheng; tel: 5166 9102; www.cnadventure.com; subway: Yonghegong; map p.135 C4
Organises hiking trips to the Great Wall.

Visas

A tourist visa is necessary for entering China and must be applied for in person or through an agent before you get to China. It is fairly easy to extend a tourist visa by a month once you are in China. If you overstay your visa there is a fairly hefty daily fine.

Visa Section, Public Security Bureau; 2 Andingmen Dongdajie (East of the Lama Temple), Dongchen; tel: 8402 0101; Mon–Sat 8.30am–4.30pm; subway: Yonghegong; map p.135 C4

Below: a picture-postcard postage stamp.

Festivals

Although Mao and materialism have diluted many of China's imperial traditions, the nation's public holidays are still split between Communist history and ancient festivals. The most important holiday is Spring Festival – New Year according to the lunar calendar – when parks and streets are decked with red lanterns, firecrackers thunder day and night, and families get together. These days, traditional Western festivals such as Christmas and Valentine's Day are also enthusiastically celebrated by young urbanites. But whatever the festival, it is invariably an excuse to go out and have a big slap-up meal.

Spring Festival (Chinese New Year)

Late Jan or early Feb

The most important traditional festival is Chinese New Year or Spring Festival (Chunjie). If you travel in China at this time, expect restricted and crowded public transport services; this is the time when everyone heads to their hometown. Trains will be fully booked, and flight tickets typically double in price. On New Year's Eve, the entire family gathers for a special meal. In Beijing and the north, families make and eat *jiaozi* (pasta parcels filled with minced meat and vegetables).

At midnight, they welcome the New Year with a volley of firecrackers – more so since a 10-year ban on fireworks was lifted in 2006.

The first day is taken up with meals and visits to relatives. The second and third days are for friends and acquaintances. People visit each other, always taking food, drink or other gifts, and offering good wishes for the New Year. During Spring Festival, many Beijing parks and temples hold fairs where you can see stilt-walkers, dragon-dancers, wrestlers, jugglers and opera singers, although

most these days are more geared towards selling plastic knick-knacks and snacks. Some of the best fairs are held in **Ditan Park** *(see p.97)*, the **New Summer Palace** *(see p.90–3)* and **Baiyunguan Temple** *(see p.122–3)*. **Longtan Park** *(see p.98)* hosts an annual spectacular national folk arts competition.

The end of celebrations is marked by the **Lantern Festival** on the 15th day of the first month in the lunar calendar, although now it is a normal working day. Only the meal of *yuanxiao* (sticky rice balls, usually filled with sweet red bean or sesame paste) follows the old customs.

Festival of Light

First week of Apr

The Festival of Light (Qingming) was originally a day to celebrate the renewal of life in springtime. Later it became a day to remember the dead. In the past, those who could afford it would make a pilgrimage to the graves of their ancestors, taking cooked chicken, pork, vegetables, fruit, incense and candles.

Left and bottom left:
New Year's celebrations.

salty meats but is sometimes sweet. The festival's origins lie in the story of poet **Qu Yuan**, who drowned on this day around 2,300 years ago as a protest against corruption. Onlookers tried to save him from flesh-eating fish by beating drums to scare them away and throwing dumplings into the water to tempt them away. You will have to head for the suburbs to see dragon boat races in Beijing – it is much more of a major spectacle in the south of the country and in Hong Kong.

Moon Festival

Late Sept or Oct

The Moon Festival or Mid-Autumn Festival (Zhongqiu-jie), is enthusiastically celebrated by the eating of moon cakes filled with various combinations of meat, fruit, beans, salted egg and lotus paste. The cakes are to remind people of the revolt against Mongol rule in the 14th century, when similar cakes were used to transport secret messages between Chinese leaders. Parents buy their children colourful lanterns, and everyone stays up past midnight to look at the moon.

In 2008, public holidays were rearranged in an effort to re-emphasise traditional celebrations at the expense of the week-long Communist holiday of Labour Day in May. The changes were also designed to ease traffic logjams that built up during 'Golden Week' holidays. Chinese New Year and National Day (a week starting 1 Oct to mark the founding of the People's Republic of China) remained as before. These are not good times to visit. Labour Day was shaved from a week to a single day, while the Qing-ming, Dragon Boat and Mid-Autumn festivals were all given a day each.

Many people, especially in rural areas, have resumed the customs of sweeping graves and burning paper money. In Beijing, schoolchildren lay wreaths and flowers in Tiananmen Square in memory of those who gave their lives for the revolution.

Dragon Boat Festival

June

The Chinese eat *zongzi* (glutinous rice dumplings, pyramid-shaped and wrapped in bamboo or reed) for the Dragon Boat Festival (Duan-wujie). The rice inside is usually stuffed with beans and

They would burn paper money, often printed with the words 'Bank of Hell', and sometimes paper clothes, furniture and houses to ensure their ancestors fared well in the spirit world. After the sacrifice, the cleaning of the graves would begin.

Right: Moon Festival celebrations carry on late into the night.

Film

China's film industry has come a long way since 1913 when its first home-grown movie, *Nanfu Nanqi*, a 45-minute short about forced marriages, was released. Zhang Yimou's *Hero* was a box-office hit in the US in 2002, and Chinese directors and actors are slowly gaining international recognition, a few even flirting with Hollywood – actresses Gong Li and Zhang Ziyi both starred in the 2005 romantic drama *Memoirs of a Geisha*. Art-house directors are frequently fêted at Cannes and other film festivals, and Beijing is one of the best places to pick up subtitled DVDs of their works.

Mainland Chinese Cinema

Pre-1949, the Chinese movie industry, largely based in Shanghai, was heavily influenced by American cinema, and comedies and martial arts flicks were standard. After the Communist revolution, movies were considered great propaganda tools, filmmakers were sent to study in Russia, and the centre of the country's movie industry shifted from Shanghai to Beijing with the establishment of the prestigious **Beijing Film Academy**. In the mid-1980s, along with the opening and reform period, the so-called 'fifth

Some movies filmed in Beijing to look out for include the marvellous *Beijing Bicycle*, which is beautifully shot in the city's hutong. *Lost in Beijing*, which while banned can still be found in DVD stores across the city, shows a grittier, more depressing capital of apartment blocks, concrete flyovers and sleazy massage parlours. Jia Zhangke's *The World* is slow and gloomy, but is expertly shot in a Beijing suburban amusement park.

generation' of film directors brought Chinese film to the attention of the international festival circuit. Two of these, **Zhang Yimou** (*Red Sorghum*, *Raise the Red Lantern*, *Hero*, *Not One Less*), and **Chen Kaige** (*Yellow Earth*, *Farewell My Concubine*) are China's most famous directors today. Their work was celebrated for its range of style and its break from the socialist realism of the Mao era. After the Tiananmen crackdown of 1989, several directors moved overseas.

By the mid-nineties, a new breed of directors, called the 'sixth generation', had emerged. Their work is distinct from their predecessors' as being edgier, grittier and more budget in production, almost documentary-like. Some names from this movement include **Wang Xiaoshuai** (*Beijing Bicycle*), **Jia Zhangke** (*Platform*, *The World*) and **Li Yang** (*Blind Shaft*). Their movies are raw, exposing the ugly side to modern 'capitalist' China – prostitution, poverty, drugs, infidelities and injustice.

The work of these independent filmmakers goes

largely unnoticed at home; it is the slapsticks and thrillers such as *Green Hat*, *Crazy Stone* and *Curiosity Kills the Cat* that get Chinese bums on seats. Big period epics such as Peter Chan's *The Warlords* (2007), Zhang Yimou's *Curse of the Golden Flower* (2006) and Chen Kaige's *The Promise* (2005) are liked by both the government and foreign moviegoers but are not so hot with the Chinese public.

Censorship

China's film directors' harshest critics are the country's censors, who are not only looking for politically provocative material but also scenes of sex and violence, chopping anything that shows China in a bad light. In 2007, Li Yu's *Lost in Beijing* had 20 minutes deleted for its sex and gambling scenes and shots of Beijing that made the city look 'dirty'. Finally the movie was completely axed in 2008 because banned scenes had been circulating on the Internet. Producers and directors

Right: *House of Flying Daggers.*

Left: a scene from *Curse of the Golden Flower*.

Cherry Lane Movies
3-2 Zhangzizhong Lu (Yugong Yishan), Dongcheng; tel: 6404 2711; www.yugongyishan.com; subway: Zhangzizhonglu; map p.134 C2
The best place to see art-house Chinese movies with English subtitles.

Cultural Office of the Mexican Embassy
Sanlitun Dong 5 Jie, Chaoyang; tel: 6532 2574; subway: Gongti Beilu; map p.135 E3

French Cultural Centre
18 Gongren Tiyuchang Xilu, Chaoyang; tel: 6553 2627; subway: taxi from Chaoyangmen; map p.135 D2

Instituto Cervantes
1 Gongren Tiyuchang Nanlu, Chaoyang; tel: 5879 9666; subway: Gongti Beilu; map p.135 E1

Italian Embassy Cultural Centre
Sanlitun Dong 2 Jie, Sanlitun, Chaoyang; tel: 6532 2187; subway: Gongti Beilu; map p.135 E2

Star City
Oriental Plaza, Wangfujing Dajie, Dongcheng; tel: 8518 6778; www.xfilmcity.com; subway: Wangfujing; map p.136 B4

UME International Cineplex
44 Kexueyuan Nanlu, Shuangyushu, Haidian; tel: 8211 5566; www.bjume.com; subway: Wudaokou

that annoy the state Film Bureau are regularly barred from making films for up to five years at a time. But this 'banned in China' status, ironically, gives underground directors the kind of kudos that the international festival applauds.

The pirate DVD shops are pretty swift at keeping up with international releases, but only 20 films a year are allowed to be commercially released in Chinese cinemas. Those movies that pass the censors are usually innocuous Hollywood blockbusters.

Cinemas

Cinema tickets are expensive – around RMB50 – and so most urban Chinese prefer to watch television or pirated DVDs – which got for about RMB8 a pop – at home. Even so, there are several big multiplexes around town; note that locally made movies are unlikely to have subtitles. If they are showing a foreign movie, check first that it hasn't been dubbed into Chinese. The cultural centres of the French, Italian, Spanish and Mexican embassies often show movies. Several bars, including **Club Obiwan** *(see p.83)* have themed film evenings when they screen DVDs. See listings magazines *That's Beijing* and *City Weekend* for what's on.

Food and Drink

The importance attached to eating in China is expressed in everyday speech: a common greeting is *chi guo le ma*? or *chi fan le ma*? (Have you eaten?). The capital's cuisine has traditionally existed in two largely separate forms; the imperial food of the royal court, which gave birth to such classics as Peking Duck, and the home-style cooking enjoyed by the ordinary citizen. Western palates generally have little difficulty adjusting to, and thoroughly enjoying, Chinese cooking – and there are few better places than Beijing for sampling it. *For specific listings see Restaurants, p.100–9.*

Beijing Cuisine

THE IMPERIAL KITCHEN

Over the centuries, the finest chefs were attracted to the imperial court, and the best among them could count on being given the rank of minister. In the palace kitchens, cooks created dishes that belonged at the pinnacle of world cuisine, dishes made from rare ingredients and prepared with great culinary skill. This is where dishes that belong to every sophisticated Chinese kitchen originated: Peking Duck, Phoenix in the Nest, Mandarin Fish, Lotus Prawns, Mu Shu Pork and Thousand Layer Cake, among others.

FEEDING THE THOUSANDS

In contrast, the traditional cuisine of the capital's workers, peasants and soldiers was simple, with plenty of onions and garlic. The variety of vegetables available further south in China was lacking – in winter, it was common to see nothing but cabbages filling the markets.

Above: making noodles.

Improved transportation and the widespread use of greenhouses means that today's residents can get pretty much anything they need, albeit at a higher price.

MIXING OF THE TRADITIONS

Beijing's modern cuisine is a mixture of these two traditions, allied to influences from across the country. The main meal of a family of four usually consists of rice, noodles or steamed bread, soup and three or four freshly prepared hot dishes. Many families will eat three cooked

meals a day, which makes for a lot of domestic work; many working people – especially those on lower incomes – eat in workplace canteens.

Eating Out

The most famous local dish is unquestionably Peking Duck *(see 'Beijing's Signature Dish, right)*, but many other culinary styles and specialities have found fame here. Traditional Beijing haute cuisine is said to reflect two styles of cooking: imperial, which is based on Qing-dynasty palace dishes; and Tan, named after the Tan family, a synthesis of salty northern cuisine with sweeter southern cuisine.

For northern China's *laobaixing* (ordinary people; literally, 'old hundred names'), the most common specialities are *jiaozi* (meat-and vegetable-filled pasta parcels), *baozi* (steamed buns stuffed with minced-meat and vegetables), noodles, cornbread and pancakes – rice is not grown in the harsh climate of the north. Stir-fried and boiled

Full duck banquets don't come cheap; in fact, they are too expensive for most Chinese families, and reserved for special occasions. There are a number of cheaper duck restaurants in Beijing, but sadly many have become pure mass-production centres.

it: very thin pancakes, little sesame-seed rolls, spring onions and *haixian* (or hoisin) sauce, a sweetish bean sauce flavoured with garlic and spices.

An authentic meal of Peking Duck begins with a selection of appetisers, most of which derive from various parts of the duck: fried liver, deep-fried heart with coriander, intestines, boiled tongues and the webbed skin of the feet cut very finely – in Chinese cooking, little is wasted. Next, the cook brings the roast duck to the table and cuts it into bite-sized pieces of skin and meat. Take one of the pancakes, use the chopped spring onion to spread *haixian* sauce on it and put a piece of duck over the spring onion. Then roll the whole

dishes often feature cabbage and potatoes.

Hotpot, sometimes called Mongolian hotpot – although Mongolians claim it originated in Korea – is another speciality. This combines fondue-style cooking – usually in a communal hotpot – with unlimited meat and vegetables. A newer challenger has also caught on: Sichuan 'yin-yang'

hotpot, divided into two compartments. Beware the fiery yang half.

Beijing's Signature Dish
A SLOW GRILL

A prerequisite for true **Peking Duck** is a special kind of duck bred in and around Beijing, which is force-fed for about six months before it is slaughtered. Preparing the duck so that it has the perfect, world-renowned melt-in-the-mouth crispness requires great skill. After slaughter, plucking and cleaning, air is carefully blown through a hole in the neck, so that the skin is loosened from the flesh. This process helps to make the skin as crisp as possible after roasting. The duck is then painted with a mixture of honey, water and vinegar and hung up to dry for three days. Afterwards, still hanging, it is slowly grilled in a special oven.

WRAPPING THE MEAT

Equally important to the Peking Duck experience are the dishes served alongside

'Thousand-Year-Old' Eggs *(pidan)* remain one of Beijing's most popular appetisers. These are duck eggs that have been packed raw into a mass of mud, chalk and ammonia and left for two weeks or so – not a thousand years. When fully preserved, the egg white turns a transparent, dark-greenish black, and the yolk turns milky yellow-green. The eggs are then cut into wedges, sprinkled with soy sauce and sesame oil, and served with pickled ginger. To many Westerners the taste is an acquired one, but nonetheless worth trying at least once.

Below: street food is cheap, delicious, safe and everywhere.

F

Left: Beijingers shop for fresh produce daily.

Gastronomic Melting Pot

Beijing has assimilated food from many Chinese regions into its *jia chang cai* (home-style dishes). These are the standard dishes you will find in restaurants and homes. Sichuan, Guangdong (Canton), Dongbei (the northeast), Shanghai, Shandong and Hunan are some of the regions that continue to influence typical Beijing menus. Milder Sichuan dishes, such as *mapo doufu* (spicy tofu) and *gongbao jiding* (stir-fried chicken with peppers and peanuts, a firm Westerner favourite), can be found in most large restaurants. Sizzling rice-crust, called *guoba*, also originated in Sichuan.

Beijing also has many restaurants specialising in the stir-fries and rice dishes from Guangdong in the deep south, universally known as 'Chinese' to the rest of the world. You can eat lean, grilled mutton and beef at restaurants run by China's Korean and Uighur minorities. The Uighurs, from Xinjiang in China's far northwest, make flatbreads and kebabs similar to those found in the Middle East. Hand-cut, stir-fried pasta pieces served in spicy tomato sauce, called *chaopian'r*, are another Xinjiang speciality. Xinjiang restaurants are easily spotted; they often have green signs, sometimes written in Arabic, and arched windows. Restaurants run by Dai (from Yunnan), Mongolian and Tibetan people offer further tastes of China's remote frontiers.

Thanks to the number of Chinese travelling abroad and the number of Westerners coming to China, there are now also a large number of Western restaurants in Beijing. Some of these are fast-food joints familiar the world over; others are more sophisticated – it is possible to find quite good French, Italian, Middle Eastern and many other types of international cuisine around the city.

Street Food

For a quick breakfast try *jidan guan bing* (egg pancakes), sold at roadside stalls. Or sample *youtiao*, deep-fried bread sticks (like doughnuts) usually eaten with *hot dou jiang* (soy milk).

Street food is also worth seeking out at other times of the day. Look out for *xian'r bing* (meat-filled pancakes), wonton soup, *jiaozi* and *baozi*.

The Dong'anmen Night Market *(see p.6)* just off Wangfujing is a good place to try regional specialities, such as skewers of spiced meat *(kaorou chuan'r)*, but there are street-food vendors

thing up and eat it using your fingers. It is this combination that provides the highest gastronomic pleasure and makes the often rather fatty meat digestible. For the final course, you will be served a soup made of the remains of the duck – mostly bones.

> **Tips on Etiquette**
> If you are invited into someone's home to eat, it is usual to bring a gift – alcohol, cigarettes, or small presents typical of your home country. Take care of your neighbours at the table, serving them some of the food, especially from dishes that they cannot reach easily. Remember also not to pick out the best pieces on each dish, but to take food from the side of the dish closest to you. At the meal, the host will drink toasts to the guests. *'Ganbei!'* (empty cup) means you should empty your glass in one shot, and turning your glass upside down shows that you have followed that instruction.

The names of Chinese dishes sometimes bear little relation to the ingredients but are more like fanciful snippets of poetry. Take *luda dong* for example. The direct translation is 'rolling donkey', but it's actually sweet glutinous rice balls. Here are some more: *Mapo doufu* (tofu made by a pock-marked woman): spicy tofu. *Mayi shangshu* (ants climbing a tree): minced pork and bean-thread noodles. *Fuqi feipian* (husband and wife lung slices): cold slices of peppery beef.

Above: Dong'anmen Night Market.

on many street corners all over town (less so around Tiananmen Square).

A Liking for Liquor

Alcohol is often an integral part of a Chinese meal. A warning to take care is not unwarranted here, as Chinese men often drink very strong grain liquor. The expensive Maotai, named after its place of origin, is famous, as is Wuliangye from Sichuan. Erguotou, the most popular Beijing brand, gives you 56 percent alcohol by volume for just a few kuai. Spirits are usually found in every restaurant and home, and are in special abundance at any type of official gathering. Many wealthy Beijing

businesspeople now prefer Remy Martin XO or similar luxury brandies.

Sweet liqueurs, more popular in the south of China, are also drunk, as is beer *(pijiu)*, which is a standard mealtime drink. Tsingtao is the leading brand, but Yanjing is locally made and is often a few kuai cheaper. Both are generally good.

Several Sino-French joint ventures produce passable, inexpensive wines – Dragon Seal and Dynasty among the better brands. Mineral water *(kuangquan shui)* and all the big-name soft drinks are universally available.

Chopsticks

Chopsticks, or *kuaizi*, date back thousands of years.

Although bone, ivory, gold, jade and steel have all been used, most chopsticks are now made of wood, and thrown away after each meal.

The main production area, the northeast, produces around 75 billion pairs a year from 68 million cubic metres of birch wood – enough to build a chopstick Great Wall every five years.

Food Souvenirs

Chinese supermarkets are the best and the cheapest place to buy spices – try Sichuan peppercorns *(mala)* star anise and Chinese hot mustard – sauces or dried food gifts to take home. They also stock fancily wrapped bottles of Chinese liquor, which can make interesting presents. Some chains to look out for are Jiankelong, Huapu and Wumart. One of these or their equivalent can be found on almost every major street.

Huapu

Huapu International Plaza,19 Chaoyangmenwai Avenue, Chaoyang; daily 8am–9pm; subway: Chaoyang; map p.135 D1

Left: exotic treats from Dong'anmen Night Market.

Gay and Lesbian

It's been slow in developing, but Beijing's gay and lesbian scene is now just about out of the closet. The capital boasts a rocking gay club, a lesbian bar in an ancient city wall, several drag bars, and even a kinky gay underwear store five minutes' walk from Tiananmen Square. Hate crime is refreshingly non-existent; the main pressure on gays comes from parents who are single-minded about their children having a conventional family. Provided they keep the intimacy to the bedroom, gay couples travelling together will hardly raise an eyebrow.

Gay Life in Beijing

China has a long history of homosexuality evident in its ancient poetry and art. From that background and the fact that there is little homophobia common to parts of the West and the Middle East – China is largely secular, and the local religions of Daoism and Buddhism are markedly tolerant – there is little hate crime or gay bashing in the People's Republic. Saying that, until 2001 homosexuality was considered a mental illness, and many Chinese gays and lesbians stay hidden in the

closet for fear of disappointing their family or being misunderstood. Parents usually place a lot of pressure on their children to get married and carry on the family name.

But all that is slowly changing. As a new generation comes of age, being gay is nothing shocking. Respected sexologist Li Yinhe has approached parliament four times with the idea of drafting a same-sex law, albeit without success, but the debate is out there, and the media are increasingly publishing sensitive pieces on the pressures

gays and lesbians face. Gay bars, clubs and saunas are allowed to operate much like their straight cousins, and activist groups are left alone as long as they don't get involved in politics, and are even encouraged if they work with NGOs on safe-sex education. Gay topics are still sensitive enough, however, to keep gay and lesbian characters out of television shows and Chinese movies for now.

Most Chinese gays and lesbians meet over the Internet, and there are hundreds of websites – mostly in Chinese – out there with news and personals. The most comprehensive are www.aibai.cn for gays and lesbians and www.lalabar.com, which has an online version of **Les+**, a bimonthly lesbian magazine. Both are in Chinese only. There are even professionally produced gay chat-show pod-casts produced inside Beijing. See http://blog.sina.com. cn/qafbeijing. Two English-language sources which

Left: fundraiser for Aids Awareness Day.

Left: a quiet drink.

Shanmulan

3 Shajing Hutong (off Nanluogu Xiang); Dongcheng; tel: 6403 7856; daily 2pm–late; subway: Gulou; map p.134 B3

This Xinjiang-inspired lesbian bar has a rooftop garden, and a cosy feel to its second floor with Islamic-arched windows and sofas. A friendly place to have a quiet drink.

Urban Love Island Bar (Qingdao in Chinese)

6 Liulichang Dongjie; Xuanwu; tel: 8316 1284; daily 8pm–1am; subway: Hepingmen; map p.139 E3

The main attraction here is the fabulous drag show. The bar is a warts-and-all peanut-shells-on-the-floor kind of gay bar, incongruously sitting at the end of the touristy Liulichang lane, and the crowd is very local.

West Wing

Deshengmen, Xicheng; tel: 8208 2836; daily 2pm–2am; subway: Jishuitan; map p.133 E4

The owner of this cute bar has some serious *guanxi* (connections), since not only does she have permission to run a bar inside an ancient city wall but a lesbian bar at that. West Wing is a mishmash of sofas, karaoke and cats, and often attracts a more mature crowd.

Promen is a popular gay social networking group in Beijing for English-speaking professional men. They have been meeting every Thursday night for cocktails since late 2006. Their evenings regularly attract around 100 men. They have a yahoo group at http://groups.yahoo.com/group/promen.

---

cover China are www.fridae.com and www.utopia-asia.com.

Local slang for gay is *tongzhi*, which literally means 'comrade', while the girls call themselves *lala*. The Chinese word for homosexual is *tongxinglian* (literally same-sex love), while bisexual is *shuangxinglian*.

Bars and Clubs

Destination

7 Gongti Xilu, Chaoyang; tel: 6551 5138; www.bj destination.com; daily 8pm–late; admission charge; subway: Chaoyangmen; map p.135 D2

This gay dance club, very popular with both locals and expatriates, has a bouncy dance floor, some decent DJs, MTV, and lots of dark

nooks to explore. It's fun and friendly, but weekends get very packed.

L'Étage

Tongli Studios, Sanlitun, Chaoyang; tel: 6416 4549; daily 7pm–late; subway: Gongti; map p.135 E2

This deep-red wine bar has a cosy atmosphere, a little terrace and more than 50 different French wines. Clientele is mixed, but gay owner Franck Bianchi hopes to encourage more gay-themed events. So far, the bar hosts lesbian movie nights on its big screen on Sundays.

Pipe

Gongti Nanlu; Chaoyang; tel: 6593 7756; Sat only 8pm–2am; admission charge; subway: taxi from Choayangman; map p.135 D1

Qiao Qiao, a young lesbian pop singer, started her Saturday night club for the ladies more than five years ago. Pipe is bit tacky, but it is the only place to find lots of dancing and drinking lesbians on a Saturday night. The crowd is mainly local and youngish (late teens and early twenties).

A sign of how far Beijing has come in accepting homosexuality is the fact that gay Singaporean Kenneth Tan obtained permission to open a closet-sized underwear store aimed at gay men literally around the corner from the seat of government at Zhongnanhai. **MANifesto** (57 Nanchizi Dajie, Tue–Sun 2–10pm) has funky briefs from the hottest homo labels, albeit on the 'small' side, jock straps, and gladiator-style lycra body suits.

History

c.3000 BC
Neolithic villages are established in the area around present-day Beijing.

c.700 BC
Trading between the Chinese, Koreans, Mongols and northern tribes starts to take place around the site of the modern city.

475–221 BC
BC Warring States period. Rise of the city of Ji, the forerunner of Beijing.

221 BC
Qin Shi Huangdi unifies China to found the first imperial dynasty, and creates the Great Wall. Beijing (still known as Ji) becomes the administrative centre of Guangyang prefecture.

AD 907–60
Beijing (called Yanjing or Nanjing) becomes the southern capital of the new Khitan (Mongol) empire under the Liao dynasty.

1153
Beijing (Zhongdu) becomes the new capital under the Nüzhen, another Mongol tribe, who overthrow the Liao to begin the Jin dynasty.

1215
Genghis Khan destroys the city.

1267
Kublai Khan starts construction of Khanbaliq, known in Chinese as Dadu (Great Capital), using Confucian ideals. An imperial palace is built in today's Beihai Park.

1279
Mongol armies establish the Yuan dynasty, reinstating Beijing as capital. Trade along the Silk Road flourishes.

1368
Han Chinese overthrow the Mongols. Ming dynasty is founded. Dadu is renamed Beiping ("Northern Peace"), and the capital is moved south to Nanjing.

1403
Beiping reinstated as capital of the empire by the emperor Yongle.

1406–20
During Yongle's reign the city is rebuilt around the new Imperial Palace and its basic layout is established.

1644
The Manchu, a non-Han Chinese people from Manchuria, seize Beijing, to initiate the Qing dynasty.

1851–64
The Taiping Rebellion.

1900
The Boxer Rebellion.

1911
Republican Revolution: Sun Yat-sen is chosen president, but he soon steps down. Abdication of the last Chinese emperor, Pu Yi.

1919
On 4 May in Beijing, a large demonstration demands the restoration of China's sovereignty, thus beginning a Nationalist movement.

1921
Founding of the Communist Party in Shanghai.

1945
Japan defeated in World War II; full-scale civil war ensues in China.

1949
Mao Zedong declares People's Republic in Beijing on 1 Oct.

1958–61
Mass famine kills over 30 million.

1960
Political split between China and Soviet Union.

1965–6
Cultural Revolution begins.

1972
President Richard Nixon visits China.

1976
Zhou Enlai (Jan) and Mao Zedong (Sept) die.

1978
Deng Xiaoping becomes leader, instituting a policy of economic reform and openness to the West.

1979
The US formally recognises China. Democracy Wall movement crushed.

1989
Pro-democracy demonstrations in Tiananmen Square brought to an end by a brutal military crackdown on 4 June.

1997
Deng Xiaoping dies.

2001
Beijing is named host city of the 2008 Olympic Games. China joins the World Trade Organization.

2003
Hu Jintao becomes president.

2005
China revalues its currency against the US dollar and moves to an exchange-rate system that references a basket of currencies.

2006
The first Beijing–Lhasa train completes the journey to Tibet.

2007
China becomes the second-largest economy in the world after the US.

2008
Beijing prepares to host the Olympics amid protests from overseas about its poor human rights record and criticisms of its handling of protests in Tibet.

Hotels

Beijing is on the map and has the hotels to prove it. There has been a boom in hotel construction, with some spectacular new or refurbished five-stars as well as an increase in the number of boutique venues and courtyard guesthouses. Many of the most palatial hotels, some with glass fronts, rotating rooftop restaurants or classical Chinese adornments, are now prominent landmarks on the city's skyline. The top end of accommodation does not come cheap, of course, but local three-star hotels and courtyard residences are often great value for money.

Along Chang'an Jie

Beijing International Hotel
9 Jianguomennei Dajie, Dongcheng; tel: 6512 6688; www.bih.com.cn/enviews/index.aspx; $$$; subway: Jianguomen; map p. 137 C4

This imposing tower of a hotel is a Beijing landmark; it opened back in 1987. While perhaps not quite deserving of its five stars most guests are pretty happy with room size, location and service. Renovation work is chipping away at the older and mustier parts of the hotel. All in all, not a bad choice and the revolv-

ing restaurant up top gives great views of Chang'an Jie.

Grand Hyatt Beijing
Oriental Plaza, 1 Dongchang'an Jie, Doncheng; tel: 8518 1234; www.beijing.grand.hyatt.com; $$$$; subway: Wangfujing; map p.136 B4

The Grand Hyatt is one of Beijing's top hotels and is in a great location at the southern end of Wangfujing in the Oriental Plaza complex. As well as 695 lushly decorated rooms, the hotel's amenities are top-notch, including its spa and prize-winning **Made in China** restaurant. The hotel's giant pool is disguised as a tropical island with whirlpools and mini-waterfalls. SEE ALSO RESTAURANTS, P.101

Haoyuan Hotel
53 Shijia Hutong (off Dongsi Nandajie), Dongcheng; tel: 6512 5557; www.haoyuanhotel.com; $$; subway: Dengshikou; map p.134 C1

The Haoyuan's 19 rooms were getting an Olympic spruce-up at the time of writing, which bodes well for this beautiful courtyard hotel. It is has a

Left: Raffles' interior.

much more open and 'temple-like' feel than its competitors. The superior rooms have traditional rosewood furniture and a Jacuzzi in the bathroom.

Hotel Côté Cour SL
70 Yanle Hutong, Dongcheng; tel: 6512 8020; www.hotelcotecoursl.com; $$$; subway: Dengshikou; map p.134 C1

Côté Cour SL is the new darling of boutique courtyard hotels and as such is a little more expensive than its rivals. Its 14 rooms are set around a beautiful courtyard with a lily pond and are gloriously decked out in traditional silks and deep wood. Breakfast in their funky dining room – look

gin and tonics in the drawing room and fawning service. This beautiful French colonial building has been a hotel since the early 1900s.

Sihe Hotel

5 Dengcao Hutong (off Dongsi Nandajie), Dongcheng; tel: 5169 3555; www.sihehotel.com; $$; subway: Dongsi; map p.134 C1

This courtyard hotel is a warren of rooms that was once the former residence of Beijing Opera star Mei Lanfang (see p.34). Sihe has a slightly cloistered air and there are reports of it being quite chilly in winter, but rooms are modern and beautifully furnished with Chinese period pieces.

Southern Beijing

Chang Gong Youth Hostel

11 Yingtaoxie Jie, Xuanwu; tel: 5194 8204; $; subway: Qianmen; map p.136 A2

This 200-year-old courtyard building, sandwiched between Dashanlan and Liulichang, has a 1920s atmosphere with its quaint central conservatory piled with plants, old furniture and goldfish. The rooms are simple but come with attached shower and a television. The staff are helpful and can arrange airport transfers and

out for the giant red door – is included in the price.

Hotel Kapok

16 Donghuamen Dajie, Dongcheng; tel: 6525 9988; www.hotel kapok.com; $$–$$$; subway: Wangfujing; map p.136 B4

In the world of Beijing boutique hotels, Kapok is something completely different. The exterior wall lattice glows green while the lobby is all glass, bamboo and curves. There's a small gym, bar, restaurant and an unusual 'sloping' reading lounge. Rooms, while a little on the small side, have wooden floors, IKEA-esque furnishings, cable television and power showers. With lots of light and open space and just a five-minute walk from the Forbidden City, Kapok is a funky choice.

The Peninsula Beijing

8 Jinyu Hutong (off Wangfujung), Dongcheng; tel: 8516 2888; www.beijing.peninsula. com; $$$$; subway: Wangfujing; map p.136 B4

This newly renovated, award-winning hotel is luxurious with a capital 'L'. All rooms have hardwood floors and 42-inch

plasma TVs. The lobby is full of Chinese antiques, while designer labels compete in the shopping arcade. It's a short walk to Wangfujing, Tiananmen Square and the Forbidden City.

Raffles Beijing Hotel

33 Chang'an Dongdajie, Dongcheng; tel: 6526 3388; beijing.raffles.com; $$$$; subway: Wangfujing; map p.136 B4

Raffles is *the* name in colonial elegance, and the 171 luxury rooms and suites attended by an army of staff resplendent in cream will not disappoint those who hanker after

Many of Beijing's luxury hotels are in the Central Business District around Guo Mao, the area around the Lufthansa Centre at the city end of the Airport Expressway, and Financial Street in the west of the city. Another hotel zone, catering to tourists as well as business travellers, is around Wangfujing and Houhai – this is a lot closer in and within walking distance of the Forbidden City and Tiananmen Square. This area has also seen a rise in the number of quaint courtyard hotels which, while not providing the luxuries of a five-star hotel, do offer a particular traditional Beijing experience.

tours. Best of all, breakfast is served in the conservatory.

Qianmen Jianguo Hotel
175 Yongan Lu, Xuanwu; tel: 6301 6688; www.qianmen hotel.com; $$$; subway: Hepingmen; map p.136 A2
This well-established three-star hotel is popular with tour groups, possibly because of its on-site Beijing Opera theatre. It is a bit out of the way in the south of the city, but it gets good reviews for its friendly service and is not far from the Temple of Heaven.

Right: Lusongyuan Hotel.

The Lake District
Red Lantern House
5 Zhengjue Hutong, Xicheng; tel: 6611 5771; $; subway: Jishuitan; map p.133 E3
A one-stop friendly back-packer shop in a hard-to-find hutong just west of Houhai. The Zhengjue Hutong court-yard has simple rooms and dorms with shared bath-rooms around a central hall that is stacked with books, plants and bric-a-brac. Around the corner, adjacent to Baoyuan Hotel, is a sep-arate courtyard that lacks some of the topsy-turvy charm of Zhengjue but has clean, modern, motel-style rooms with attached bath-room in a courtyard of per-simmon trees.

Sleepy Inn
103 Deshengmen Daijie (on Xihai), Xicheng; tel: 6406 9954; www.sleepyinn.com.cn; $; subway: Jishuitan; map p.133 E3
Sleepy Inn has one of the nicest budget views in town, overlooking the willow-lined Xihai Lake. Rooms are func-tional and clean, with white linen, pine furniture and trad-itional Chinese floral print covering the windows. Very backpacker-friendly, with

organised tours, Internet and a little restaurant.

Xinyuan Inn
21 Yandai Xiejie, Xicheng; tel: 6401 4753; $; subway: Gulou; map p.134 A3
This new little boutique lodge on a lane leading to Houhai offers big sunny rooms neatly furnished in Chinese dark-wood and red silks, with some good views of the tiled eaves of neighbouring hutong. The only downside is the bathrooms, which while modern and glass-walled, are a little snug. Not a courtyard residence as such, it does have a rooftop garden and nice touches in the rooms, such as portraits of Beijing opera stars. The 'honeymoon suite' has Qing-dynasty-style four-poster beds. Xinyuan is Beijing's best-value traditional-style option.

Gulou
Beijing Bamboo Garden Hotel
24 Xiaoshiqiao Hutong, Jiugulou Dajie, Xicheng; tel: 6403 2229; www.bbgh.com.cn; $$; subway: Gulou; map p.134 A3
One of Beijing's most atmos-pheric hotels is set in a grand courtyard in a hutong just north of the Drum Tower. It was the former villa of Sheng

Left: most staff at the larger hotels speak English.

Xuanhuai, an official of the latter Qing court. The classical Chinese garden has bamboo groves, covered corridor-walkways, and ponds. Rooms are well equipped with bathtub, a desktop computer with Internet access, flat-screen TV and mini bar. There's a beautiful tea house, business centre and restaurant.

Guxiang20
20 Nanluogu Xiang, Dongcheng; tel: 6400 5566; www.guxiang 20.com; $$–$$$; subway: taxi from Gulou; map p.134 B3

This elegant hotel goes heavy on the traditional Chinese – think teapots and red silk – but rooms are large and sunny, and there's a tennis court on the roof. Guxiang20 lacks the relaxed friendliness of the courtyard hotels but is new, efficient and has a chilled bar.

Hutong Ren
71 Ju'er Hutong (off Nanluogu Xiang), Dongcheng; tel: 8402 5238; $–$$; subway: taxi from Gulou; map p.134 B3

This cosy jumble of rooms is tucked into a little hutong just off Nanluogu Xiang. Rooms are simply but lovingly decorated – each one with potted plants, a squashy sofa, bookshelves full of books, Chinese floral prints and a modern bathroom. The staff are friendly, the attached coffee shop has wi-fi, and there's a small atrium with a tree growing out of the skylight. Beijing's best budget choice by far.

Lama Temple Youth Hostel
56 Beixinqiao Toutiao (off Yonghegong Dajie), Dongcheng; tel: 6402 8663; $; subway: Beixinqiao; map p.134 C3

This relaxed and very traveller-friendly hostel – bike rental, laundry, DVDs, Internet, tour advice, muesli breakfast – is also beautifully decorated. The lobby is a throne room with painted wooden beams and porcelain. The rooms unfortunately have no natural light, windows look out onto a lobby, but are new and clean, with antique-style furniture and painted basins.

Lusongyuan Hotel
22 Banchang Hutong, Dongcheng; tel: 6401 1116; www.the-silk-road.com; $$; subway: Zhangzizhonglu; map p.134 B2

This delightful and peaceful courtyard hotel is the former Qing-dynasty residence of General Zeng Ge Ling Qin. Rooms are very attractive, with period furnishings and bathtubs, although mattresses are hard. Stone lions guard the traditional wooden gate, which leads to the pavilions, trees, rockeries and potted plants that fill the courtyards. The attention to detail is stunning. The hotel is just a few minutes' walk east from Nanluogu Xiang.

Red Capital Residence
Dongsi 6 Tiao, Dongcheng; tel: 8403 5308; www.redcapital club.com.cn; $$–$$$; subway: Zhangzizhonglu; map p.134 C2

This exclusive five-room boutique hotel is within a Qing-dynasty courtyard house

Price ranges, which are given as a guide only, are for a standard double room with bathroom per night, including service and tax but without breakfast. Note that rates can be significantly lower if booked through a travel agent or when the hotel is running a promotion.
$ under RMB500
$$ RMB500–1,000
$$$ RMB1,000–2,000
$$$$ over RMB2,000

Below: Bamboo Garden.

northeast of Wangfujing. Its rooms are furnished with period antiques and each has a different theme – the Chairman's Suite is dedicated to Mao Zedong and the Concubine's Private Courtyard purports to be for anyone who has ever dreamed of being – or having – a concubine.

7 Days Inn
47 Jiugulou Dajie, Xicheng; tel: 6405 8188; www.7days inn.cn; $; subway: Gulou; map p.134 A3
The lobby is more like an airport check-in, guests are efficiently shuttled to their rooms by headphone-wearing staff, and everything is painted in a shocking yellow or green. But 7 Days Inn is cheap, efficient

Budget Chains
People of a growing Chinese middle class, eager to see their own country, have shaken up the hotel industry, kick-starting a brigade of new budget hotel chains. In 2006, the number of domestic tourists jumped by 17 percent from a year earlier, with 1.39 billion trips generating US$85 billion. Beijing now has dozens of branches of budget-chain hotels which offer clean, modern hotel rooms for as little as RMB200 a night – a long way from the days of state-run guesthouses with cigarette burns in the carpet, stains on the wallpaper and dodgy bathrooms. They are also great places to stay if you don't have the money for a five-star but don't want to stay in a hostel. Some of the major chains to look out for are: market leader and Nasdaq-listed **Home Inn** *(Ru jia)*, **Super 8 Hotel, Huatian Inn** and **7 Days Inn** *(see Gulou listing, above).*

– rooms have wireless, modern showers, televisions and kettles. Hotel-style rooms for backpacker prices. 7 Days Inn – and other budget chains – offer the best-value rooms in the city. This branch is just north of the Drum Tower and a short walk from Houhai.

Swiss Road Hotel
48 Jianchang Hutong, Guozjianjie, Dongcheng; tel: 8400 1034; www.swissroad.com.cn; $$; subway: Andingmen; map p.134 B3
The six rooms in this tiny new hutong hotel are a hip mix of traditional Chinese and modern European. While they are well equipped – plasma television, wireless, safe, heated floors – they are a bit on the small side, and the ground-floor suites don't get much sun. The hotel is in a great location, literally around the corner from the Confucius Temple.

The Embassy District
Hilton Hotel
1 Dongfang Lu, Dongsanhuan Beilu, Chaoyang; tel: 5865 5000; www.beijing.hilton.com; $$$$; subway: taxi from Dongsishitiao or Nongzhangguan
Beijing's Hilton has built up a great reputation for its service, but like the Kempinski

(see below) it is a bit out of the way of the main tourist sites. Rooms are spacious, modern and tastefully decorated; there's even an LCD screen in the bathroom. The hotel's Zeta bar used to host gay networking events.

Holiday Inn Lido
6 Jiangtai Lu, Chaoyang; tel: 6437 6688; http://beijing-lido.holiday-inn.com; $$$
An expatriate living area has grown up around this hotel feeding off the Western shops, restaurants, cafés and bars in the building and in the neighbouring Hairun International Condominium. It is just 20 minutes from the airport and is busy, efficient and serviceable. Check out its karma-friendly **Pure Lotus** vegetarian restaurant.
SEE ALSO RESTAURANTS, P.104

Kempinski Hotel
Beijing Lufthansa Centre, 50 Liangmaqiao Lu, Chaoyang; tel: 6465 3388; $$$$; www. kempinski-beijing.com; subway: taxi from Dongsishitiao or Nongzhangguan
Not in the best location, just off the busy Third Ring Road, but relatively close to the airport. This Sino-Teutonic giant has all the comforts but little charm. If you are missing

Right: Kerry Centre.

www.beijing.swissotel.com;
$$$$; subway: Dongsishitiao;
map p.135 D2
Its semicircular, mirrored
facade dominates one of Beijing's busy intersections and
is convenient for the Sanlitun
restaurant and bar area,
although there is nothing
within immediate walking distance of the hotel. Rooms are
light, modern and airy, but
the whole hotel is a little
characterless. The fourth
floor is barrier-free for travellers with disabilities.

Price ranges, which are given
as a guide only, are for a
standard double room with
bathroom per night, including
service and tax but without
breakfast. Note that rates can
be significantly lower if
booked through a travel agent
or when the hotel is running a
promotion.
$ under RMB500
$$ RMB500–1,000
$$$ RMB1,000–2,000
$$$$ over RMB2,000

European food, its Paulaner
Brauhaus German restaur-
ant and Deli come highly
recommended.

St Regis Hotel
21 Jianguomenwai Dajie,
Chaoyang; tel: 6460 6688;
www.stregis.com; $$$$;
subway: Jiangoumen;
map p.137 D4
The St Regis – think marble,
leather armchairs and but-
lers – was undergoing a
major facelift at the time of
writing and was due to
reopen in 2008. The hotel is
in a great location, near leafy
Ritan, and its bar is a
favourite of the foreign
business community.

Swissotel Beijing
Hong Kong-Macau Centre,
2 Chaoyangmen Beidajie,
Chaoyang; tel: 6553 2288;

Central Business District
China World Hotel
1 Jianguomenwai Dajie,
Chaoyang; tel: 6505 2266;
www.shangri-la.com; $$$$;
subway: Guomao; map p.137 E4
The smooth, brown curves of
Shangri-La's China World
have been around for a
while. This opulent five-star
choice is slap bang in the
middle of the CBD and hides
some of the city's best
restaurants – such as **Aria**.
Rooms are tastefully decorated, with modern art and
moody lighting.
SEE ALSO RESTAURANTS, P.107

Jianguo Hotel
5 Jianguomenwai Dajie,
Chaoyang; tel: 6500 2233;
www.hoteljianguo.com;
$$$; subway: Yonganli;
map p.137 E4

If you don't want the pomp
and circumstance of hotels
like China World, Jianguo
offers similar levels of com-
fort but at half the price.
Rooms were renovated in
2007 and it has great facili-
ties, including a large pool
and a French restaurant. Just
down from the Silk Market
and a short taxi ride from
Sanlitun bar district, it also
garnered a following
with repeat guests.

Kerry Centre
1 Guanghua Lu, Chaoyang;
tel: 6561 8833; www.shangri-la.
com/kerrycentre; $$$$; subway:
Guomao; map p.135 E1
Aimed at business travellers
and linked to a major commer-
cial and shopping complex,
this hotel offers a full range
of facilities, from Jacuzzis
to live jazz performances,
and from movie channels to

Left: Crowne Plaza Wuzhou.

broadband Internet access. The pool is especially large. Celebrities and cocktail-lovers favour **Centro**, its cavernous lounge bar.

SEE ALSO BARS, P.33

Park Hyatt Beijing

2 Jianguomenwai Dajie, Yintai Tower, Chaoyang; tel: 8567 1234; http://beijing.park.hyatt.com; $$$$; subway: Guomao; map p.137 E4

The heights of extravagance will be reached when the Park Hyatt opens its doors, ready for the 2008 Olympics. The luxury hotel will turn the concept on its head by having the lobby on one of its top floors – the entire structure topped by a giant glass pyramid, dubbed a 'Chinese lantern' encased in a steel lattice-work. Rooms are expected to earn each one of their five stars, with heated

Price ranges, which are given as a guide only, are for a standard double room with bathroom and tax but without breakfast. Note that rates can be significantly lower if booked through a travel agent or when the hotel is running a promotion.
$ under RMB500
$$ RMB500–1,000
$$$ RMB1,000–2,000
$$$$ over RMB2,000

floors, coffee machines, a 'spa-inspired bathroom', wireless, flat-screen televisions and unrivalled views of the city.

Western Beijing

Beijing Templeside House Youth Hostel

3 Liuhe Hutong, Fuchengmennei Jie, Xicheng; tel: 6617 2571; www.templeside.com; $; subway: Fuchengmen; map p.133 D1

This cosy little hutong hostel is a 20-minute walk from the Forbidden City. In winter the rooms are chilly, but most guests are charmed by the peaceful location, the enthusiastic staff and a rooftop picnicking area. There's free wireless, help with arranging tours and Chinese cooking classes – make your own dumplings.

InterContinental Beijing Financial Street

11 Financial Street, Xicheng; tel: 5852 5888; www.intercontinental.com/icbeijing; $$$$; subway: Fuchengmen; map p.133 C1

The InterContinental was the first five-star kid on the block in Financial Street. Again, expect all the luxury that the brand promises. The only problem is unless you're doing business out here the immedi-

ate environs are a bit bleak – a busy highway and bank buildings – although it's a short taxi ride into the centre of the city.

Westin Beijing Financial Street

9B Financial Street, Xicheng; tel: 6606 8866; westin.com/beijingfinancial; $$$$; subway: Fuchengmen; map p.133 C1

The Financial Street behemoths are super-luxurious, professional and slickly run – the Westin is no exception. Its **Heavenly Spa** is magic, its infinity pool plays underwater music, and the hotel is suffused with sunlight. Expatriates swear by Sunday brunch.

SEE ALSO PAMPERING, P.95

The North

Crowne Plaza Wuzhou

8 Beisihuan Zhonglu, Chaoyang; tel: 8498 2288; $$$–$$$$; subway: Huixinxijie Beikou

The Crowne Plaza is an efficient business hotel and sits right next to the Beijing International Convention Centre. The hotel's big claim to fame is its proximity to the Olympic Village, but once the games are over though there is little reason for tourists to stay this far out.

Friendship Hotel

81 Zhongguancun Dajie, Haidian; tel: 6849 8888; www.bjfriendshiphotel.com; $$–$$$; subway: taxi from Xizhimen

This state-run hotel has been spruced up for the Olympics and appears to be good value for money, although don't expect Western-style five-star service or amenities. This used to be the place where overseas workers were put up by the government. The hotel is set in spacious grounds but is in quite a lonely part of town, surrounded by highways.

If you book through a website you can get considerable reductions on published rates. Some good reliable online agents are: **elong** (www.elong.net), **Ctrip** (http://english.ctrip.com) and **www.beijing-hotels.com**. **www.hostelworld.com** is a good resource for budget accommodation.

Above and below: Commune by the Great Wall.

Western Fringes

Beijing Fragrant Hills Mountain Yoga Retreat Centre

6 Gonfuzhen, Fragrant Hills, Haidian; tel: 8259 5335; www.mountainyoga.cn; $; pick-up at Ritan

An idyllic retreat for yoga enthusiasts or others who want a unique experience in Beijing. The guesthouse is only open from March to November. All rooms are beautifully appointed. Meals are vegetarian, and Hatha yoga classes are offered each morning, including one session on the Great Wall.

Fragrant Hills Hotel

Fragrant Hills Park, Haidian; tel: 6259 1166; $$$; subway: taxi from Xizhimen

The best thing about this hotel is its design, a gentle meld of western and Chinese architecture orchestrated by famous American-Chinese designer IM Pei. The hotel itself gets lukewarm reviews and it maybe more worthwhile to admire than to stay.

The Great Wall

Commune by the Great Wall

tel: 8118 1888; www.commune.com.cn; $$$$

Twelve spectacular villas – with equally spectacular prices – designed by Asia's top architects. Each is furnished by renowned designers and comes with a personal butler, with the Shuiguan section of the wall literally as a backdrop.

Phase 2 villas, finished in 2006, brought the Commune into the realm of a less celebrity-level budget. There's the **Anantara** spa, art, gallery, kids' club and a spread of top-notch eateries.
SEE ALSO PAMPERING, P.95

Red Capital Ranch

28 Xiaguandi Village, Yanxi Township, Huairou; tel: 8401 8886; www.redcapital club.com.cn; $$$–$$$$

This Manchurian hunting lodge nestled in the shadow of the Great Wall is luxuriously restored and filled with antiques. Guests can hike on the Wall or avail themselves of the Ranch's fine restaurant and spa.

Hutong

The heart of Beijing lies behind its modern facade, in the tranquil hutong – narrow alleys that have been the hub of the city's street life for at least 700 years. Strolling or cycling around these areas is an experience not to be missed, giving a glimpse of the city as it used to be. But since a good number of the capital's population still make their home in these webs of single-storey courtyard residences, it is also a window on the city's present. The Hutong may lack the glamour of the latest architectural constructions, but they hold many surprises of their own.

History of the Hutong

Since the time of Genghis Khan, Beijingers have built single-storey homes with tiled roofs, facing into a central courtyard and protected by high walls. They are set within a labyrinth of crumbling grey alleyways, some dating back many centuries. The origin of the word is in some dispute – one school of thought has it that it comes from the Mongolian word *hottog*, meaning 'water wall'. When hutong were first made they would have been gathered around a source of water.

The number of hutong multiplied dramatically under the Qing dynasty. The Manchus, who insisted on a separate identity, split Beijing into a northern part reserved for Manchus, while the majority Han were relegated to the southern areas. This is still evident today in the character of the hutong – those in the south are more sprawling and more commercial in nature, filled with bustling shopping districts, than the more 'elegant'

hutong north of Chang'an Jie in Dongsi and Gulou.

Life in the Hutong

Just under half of real Beijingers still live and work in Beijing's hutong. Tiny workshops dimly lit by a single bare bulb, street vendors selling steamed *baozi*, inquisitive children, old men carrying their songbirds in bamboo cages, coal smoke and bicycles – all form part of this vaguely Dickensian scene. In parts the hutong are so cramped that trees hundreds of years old emerge from skylights, and

Left: caged songbirds hang from the eaves of courtyards.

washing is hung out to dry on street signs. For those who bemoan the increasingly standardised, international facade of modern Beijing, these alleyways provide instant succour. See them before they disappear.

Hutong under Threat

As Beijing continues to modernise, the hutong are under threat. The least salubrious were cleared in the 1950s to make way for apartment blocks, but sizeable areas of courtyard houses remained until the late 1980s. As in the West, housing policies have wavered between wholesale redevelopment and sensitive renovation. Now *siheyuan* (courtyard houses) and hutong are bearing the brunt of the drive to create a modern metropolis of mirrored-glass skyscrapers and ivy-clad flyovers.

It is easy for outsiders to be sentimental about the destruction of old buildings, but the fact is that many

Left: hutong transport.

the alleys to Beijing's cultural heritage and residents to petition officials and courts. Nearly two-thirds of the 1,330 hutong that existed in Beijing in the mid-1950s have gone. Though the demolition continues, the ongoing debate seems likely to guarantee that some, at least, will survive.

Hutong Areas

There are three main areas to see hutong in Beijing. The tight knot of streets that lies immediately south of **Qianmen Gate** (map p.136 A3) are getting a battering from the developers' bulldozers, but there are still some twisting alleyways left; the area around **Houhai** and the **Bell** and **Drum Towers** (map p.134 A3) are home to a mixture of bread-and-butter homes and renovated properties developed into bars and cafés for wealthy urbanites and tourists; while the **Dongzhimen** (map p.135 C3) and **Dongsi** (map p.134 C2) lanes are probably the best for authenticity.

On the surface they all look alike, but Beijing's hutong are many and varied. **Beixinqiao Hutong** (map p.135 C3) has more than 20 bends; **Qianshi Hutong** (map p.136 A3) is only 40cm wide; **Dong Jiaomin Hutong** (map p.136 A3) is the longest at 6.5km, while **Guantong Hutong** (map p.136 A3) is the shortest at 30m.

hutong dwellings are cramped and squalid. Some are comprised of just one or two small rooms, functioning as combined kitchens, living rooms, bedrooms and washrooms. The families use a public toilet in the alley, not pleasant at the best of times, let alone in the freezing winter months. A 15th-floor apartment with all modern conveniences naturally holds great appeal.

Yet some families prefer to stay put, fearing exile to distant suburbs with poor infrastructure. Others believe hutong should be preserved for their historical value. In a country where government control normally restricts public debate to the most trivial issues, the fate of the hutong has prompted academics to write articles stressing the importance of

Enterprising locals and expats, exploiting the allure of the hutong, have established some fine restaurants in renovated courtyards. While chilly in winter, they are fabulous venues for a romantic dinner when the weather warms up. Some of the best establishments are the tumbledown **Café Sambal**, serving Malaysian cuisine, the atmospheric **Dali Courtyard**, which offers a set menu of Yunnan food, the kitsch **Private Kitchen No. 44**, with Guizhou dishes, and of course, the (some say overpriced) fusion palace, **The CourtYard** *(see also Restaurants, p.101, 106).*

Below: family members wrap up against the Beijing winter to dine together in an old courtyard.

Language

Beijingers speak Putonghua, known in the West as Mandarin Chinese. Based on the northern dialect, it is promoted as standard Chinese throughout the country, although most people also speak their local dialect. Native Beijingers, for example, also speak Beijinghua, a dialect of Putonghua. The accent in the capital is harsher than the softer southern accents, with a distinct 'er' sound added to the end of many syllables. Staff in most upscale Beijing hotels and tourist areas will be able to speak some English, but it is a good idea to write down your destination in Chinese, because taxi drivers speak little English.

Chinese Characters

Written Chinese uses tens of thousands of characters, many of which are based on ancient pictograms. Some characters used today go back 3,000 years. There are strict rules on the stroke order of writing, and children spend many hours rote learning characters. In the past the script was written from right to left and top to bottom, but now it is usually written from left to right.

Tones

In the Western sense, spoken Chinese has only 420 single-syllable root words, but four tones are used to differentiate these basic sounds. Tones make it difficult for foreigners to learn the language, since different tones give the same syllable a completely different meaning. The first tone (1) is pitched high and even, the second (2) rising, the third (3) low, and the fourth (4) falling. There is also a fifth, 'neutral' tone (-). The tones are sometimes marked above the main vowel in the syllable.

The Pinyin System

Since 1958, the pinyin system has been used to represent Chinese characters phonetically in the Latin alphabet. It is very different from the Wade-Giles system used in Taiwan. You will find many shop names and most street names written in pinyin, so it is helpful to learn the basic rules of the system.

Ao is in the 'ou' of loud
C as in the 'ts' of rats
Ei as in the 'ay' of may
I as in the 'ee' of keen
Q as in the 'ch' of cheers
U as in the 'oo' of shoot
X as in the 'sh' of sheep
Zh as in the 'j' of jungle

Left and below left: calligraphy is treated as an art form on the same level as painting or novel-writing.

Glass *Beizi* (1,-) 杯子
Bring me some tissues *Gei wo lai yi xie canjinzhi* (3,3,3,2,1,1,1,1,3) 给我来一些餐巾纸
I don't eat meat/I am a vegetarian *Wo bu chi rou* (3,4,1,4) 我不吃肉
I did not order this *Zhege wo mei dian* (4,-,3,2,3) 这个我没点
I can't eat spicy food *Wo bu hui chi lade* (3,4,4,1,4,-) 我不会吃辣的
Where is the bathroom? *Weishengjian zai nar?* (4,1,1,4,3) 卫生间在哪儿?
Cheers! *Ganbei!* (1,1) 干杯!
Bill, please *Maidan* (3,1) 买单

TRANSPORT
Airport *Jichang* (1,3) 机场
Train station *Huoche zhan* (3,1,4) 火车站
Taxi *Chuzuche* (1,1,1) 出租车
Where is...? *...zai nar?* (4,3) ...在哪儿?
North *Bei* (3) 北
South *Nan* (2) 南
East *Dong* (1) 东
West *Xi* (1) 西

EMERGENCIES
Police *Jingcha* (3,2) 警察
Hospital *Yiyuan* (1,4) 医院
I need a doctor *Wo yao kanbing* (3,4,4,4) 我要看病

While some 6,000 Chinese characters are in regular use, you only need about 3,000 to read a newspaper. Mainland China has reformed written Chinese several times since 1949, and simplified characters are now used. Hong Kong and Taiwan still use the old complex characters.

COMMON EXPRESSIONS
Hello *Ni hao* (3,3) 你好
How are you? *Ni hao ma?* (3,3,-) 你好吗?
Goodbye *Zai jian* (4,4) 再见
Sorry *Duibuqi* (4,4,3) 对不起
Thank you *Xie xie* (4,-) 谢谢
My name is... *Wo jiao...* (3,4) 我叫...
What is your name? *Ni jiao shenme?* (3,4,2,-) 你叫什么?
I am from the UK *Wo shi yingguo ren* (3,4,1,2,2) 我是英国人
OK *Xing* (2) 行

SHOPPING
How much is it? *Zhege duoshao qian?* (4,-,1,3,2) 这个多少钱?

Right: signs in English are helpful and at times amusing.

Can you make it cheaper? *Neng pianyi dianr ma?* (2,2,-,3,-) 能便宜点儿吗?
I don't want it, thank you *Buyaole, xie xie* (4,4,-,4,-) 不要了, 谢谢

FOOD
Restaurant *Can ting* (1,1) 餐厅
Waiter/waitress *Fuwuyuan* (2,4,2) 服务员
Eat *Chi fan* (1,4) 吃饭
Breakfast *Zaofan* (1,4) 早饭
Lunch *Wufan* (3,4) 午饭
Dinner *Wanfan* (3,4) 晚饭
Menu *Caidan* (4,1) 菜单
Chopsticks *Kuaizi* (4,-) 筷子
Knife *Daozi* (1,-) 刀子
Fork *Chazi* (1,-) 叉子
Spoon *Shaozi* (2,-) 勺子

71

Literature

The written word is so revered in China that calligraphy has developed into an art unto itself. Literary scholars have always garnered respect; Mao himself was a poet. Classical texts take some work to plough through, but contemporary authors, those both banned and feted in China, shed a fascinating insight on modern culture and are also increasingly being translated into English. Beijing has a vibrant book culture with several giant bookstores, many of which also offer a good selection of foreign-language titles, albeit under the restrictions of government censorship.

History of Chinese Literature

The earliest examples of Chinese literature emerged around 5,000 years ago. Writings were largely confined to philosophical and religious texts such as the *I Ching* (Book of Changes), a Daoist treatise on predicting the future. Chinese poetry reached its zenith during the Tang dynasty which nurtured such poetic greats as **Li Bai**, **Du Fu** and **Wang Wei**.

It wasn't until the Ming dynasty, that the Chinese novel emerged. Scholars have come up with a definitive quartet of the best and most influential books from this period: namely *Romance of the Three Kingdoms*; *Outlaws of the Marsh*; *Journey to the West*; and *Dream of the Red Chamber*. They have had a tremendous impact on Chinese and Asian cultures and their stories are reshaped and rehashed in a host of TV dramas, movies and computer games.

After the fall of the last dynasty, novelists largely abandoned the historical and

romantic epic and instead started writing in the vernacular and exploring political and nationalistic themes. The most famous of these was **Lu Xun**, oft called the 'father of modern Chinese literature.' He was an ardent leftist and thus his stories became favourite set texts in schools in China post-1949. Under Mao, the only literature that was allowed was Socialist Realism that aimed to promote the idea of a Communist state.

The modern Chinese novel covers ground as broad as any in the West, although if you want your book published in the People's Republic you cannot criticize the government or delve too much into

San Wei Bookstore (60 Fuxingmennei Dajie, Xichengin Fuchengmen, map p.139 D4) is a cross between a tea house and a bookstore. It stocks Chinese-language books to buy and read on the premises and hosts author talks – sadly only in Chinese. Come here Saturday night for the live traditional Chinese music performances.

the world of sex, drugs and crime. The Cultural Revolution, which is an increasingly popular topic, is now fair game. Famous banned titles include 'bad girl' prose, such as **Mian Mian**'s *Candy* and **Wei Hui**'s *Shanghai Baby*, and the 'hooligan' novels of **Wang Shuo**, which frequently explore the underbelly of Beijing's darker society.

Some of the most influential contemporary authors to look out for are **Su Tong** *(Raise the Red Lantern, Rice)* whose historical fiction delves into the darker, brutal sides of human nature; **Yu Hua** *(To Live)* whose latest novel *Brothers*, a shocking black comedy, was a best seller; and satirist **Mo Yan** *(Red Sorghum, The Republic of Wine)*, whom *Time* magazine calls the 'most widely pirated of all Chinese writers.' Also look out for **Jiang Rong**'s *Wolf Totem*. Jiang won the inaugural Man Asian Booker prize with this book in 2007 which was also a massive hit on the mainland. Penguin promises an English version.

Left: Jiang Rong and his book *Wolf Totem*.

pricier selection of English-language titles and magazines – including the *Economist* – but The Bookworm's magic is that it sells banned titles under the table, has a good range of non-fiction on China and holds book talks by China boffins.

Chaterhouse Booktrader
The Place, 9 Guanghua Road, Chaoyang; tel: 65871328; daily 10am–10pm; subway: Yonganli; map p.137 E4

Tucked away in a mall basement, this is one of Beijing's best English-language bookstores with a comparatively wide range of titles of modern fiction and popular magazines.

Foreign Languages Bookstore
235 Wangfujing Dajie, Dongcheng; tel: 6512 6911; daily 9am–9pm; subway: Wangfujing; map p.136 B4

This old favourite has the widest range of competitively-priced English-language titles in the city on its ground floor as well as good selection of Chinese study texts. While you won't be able to buy banned titles there's everything from copies of the *Koran* to the latest paperbacks on the *New York Times'* best seller lists.

Further Reading

The Chinese by Jasper Becker. Free Press 2001. After 20 years as a correspondent in Beijing, Becker offers his sharp observation of the Chinese, from politician to peasant in clean prose.

Oracle Bones: A Journey Between China and the West by Peter Hessler, John Murray 2007. Hessler is humble, witty and insightful about his time working in Beijing as a journalist.

Beijing: From Imperial Capital to Olympic City by Lillian Li, Palgrave 2007. Beijing under the looking glass from its Mongolian origins to its modern-day frenzy

The Changing Face of China: From Mao to Market by John Gittings, Oxford University Press 2006. A studiously researched and balanced overview of modern China since the death of Mao.

Bookshops

Beijing Books Building
17 Xichang'an Jie, Xicheng; tel: 6607 8477; www.bjbb.com; daily 8:30am–9pm; subway: Xidan; map p.139 E4

This behemoth of a bookstore has a reasonable stock of English language titles – including quite a lot of business and self-help non-fiction and coffee table tomes – in its basement. It's worthwhile browsing the Chinese-language best-seller displays to find out what the locals are reading.

The Bookworm
Building 4, Nansanlitun Lu, Chaoyang; tel: 6586 9507; www.beijingbookworm.com; daily 9am–2am; subway: Gongtibeilu; map p.135 E2

A mid-range and slightly

Museums and Galleries

There are more than 100 museums in Beijing and with the city's growing affluence a few of these, such as the Planetarium, are anything as good as you would encounter in the West. Even those a bit curled around the edges are quirky enough to warrant a visit: the Natural History Museum has pickled human corpses, for example. More vibrant is the capital's art scene which now boasts hundreds of galleries and funky art districts riding on the global craze for contemporary Chinese art.

A Rising Star in Art

Beijing is the most important arts centre in China and – somewhat surprisingly – is also artistically freer than many other cities. Artists find it easy to hide between the cracks of its many bureaucracies, or to play one ministry off against another in order to get approval for an avant-garde exhibition or performance.

In traditional art, painting comprises various different disciplines: calligraphy; monochromatic and coloured work in ink on fabric or paper; mural reproductions such as wood-block prints; and other related techniques, such as embroideries and woven pictures; and purely decorative paintings.

Free entertainment magazines *Beijing Time Out*, *That's Beijing*, and *City Weekend* will have museum and art gallery listings and reviews of current exhibitions. Copies are distributed freely in most hotels and western-style restaurants and bars.

Because of their close connection, painting skills are learned in much the same way as writing: through copying old masters or textbooks. A painter is considered a master of his art only when the necessary brushstrokes for a bird, a chrysanthemum or a waterfall can flow effortlessly from his hand. The strong emphasis placed on perfection quickly leads to specialisation by painters on specific subjects. In this way, for instance, **Xu Beihong** (1895–1953) became known as the painter of horses, just as **Qi Bai-Shi** (1862–1957) was famous for his shrimps.

Left: political commentary in art is not encouraged...

One of the most favoured painting forms in China is landscape painting. Notable characteristics of this form are perspectives that draw the viewer into the picture, plain surfaces (unpainted empty spaces) that add a feeling of depth, and the harmonious relationship between man and nature, with man depicted as a small, vanishing, figure.

Chinese brush painting and calligraphy are generally mounted on a hanging scroll. Oil painting was introduced by Jesuit missionaries, along with such Western painting techniques as the use of perspective. It never caught on, except as an export product, until the communist era, when it became a popular medium for producing socialist-realist art. Many of China's best-known contemporary painters also work in oil paints.

Contemporary art is big in Beijing, visible at private galleries and at performance-art exhibitions. The Beijing suburbs are home to several

Left: northern Beijing's art scene is one of the hottest in the world.

Museum and dozens of downtown galleries there are stylish galleries opening around the city and at least five art districts in the suburbs – **Factory 798** in Dashanzi, the **Liquor Factory**, **Caochangdi**, **Songzhuang** and the **East End Arts District**. Of these 798 is the most established, some say commercialized, mixing the galleries with hip little bistros and bars.

You can pick up good print reproductions of famous works, both traditional and contemporary, for as little as RMB400 from the art shops across from the National Art Museum and tourist markets such as **Silk Street**.
SEE ALSO SHOPPING, P.112

Beijing will make all museums free by 2009. But before then the **Beijing Museum Voucher** gives free or half-price entry for the majority of the city's museums for a flat fee of RMB80. Since entrance fees are around RMB30 a pop, the voucher is only worth it if you plan to visit more than three. Note, many of Beijing's museums are closed on Mondays.

colonies of artists from around the country, although the life of these colonies tends to be short-lived, since they are usually torn down by real-estate developers or abandoned by artists who have grown rich from selling their paintings to foreigners. The contemporary art scene has moved rapidly through styles, including pop art and a horrific mid-1990s focus on 'body art', which involved the use of corpses and body pieces as art materials. In recent years, the trend is toward installations, film and video.

Beijing's main art event is the **Dangdai International Art Festival** (DIAF, www.diaf.org).

While the festival started off in Factory 798, since 2007 it has spread to several of the art districts, downtown galleries and even theatres. The festival usually takes place in September and October.

Censorship

Artists generally have a lot more freedom from control than writers in China but there are certain topics that are definitely taboo. They include negative depictions of Mao Zedong, or any Chinese political leaders for that matter, and anything to do with the Tiananmen protests. In 2006, for example, a painting by Gao Qiang of Mao, his skin a pallid yellow, lolling about in a river of blood, was ordered removed from a Dashanzi gallery. Nudity and sexually explicit works, on the other hand, are usually tolerated.

Galleries

There is no shortage of places to see art in Beijing. As well as the **National Art**

Along Chang'an Jie

National Art Museum
1 Wusi Dajie (just north of Wangfujing), Dongcheng; tel: 6400 6326; www.namoc. org; daily 9am–5pm; entrance fee; subway: Wangfujing; map p.134 B1
While there is a heavy emphasis on traditional art, this large pleasant gallery has been growing ever more inventive with exhibitions from kite design to Magritte.

Right: ...but nudity and sex is overlooked.

75

The area around the museum is full of character. Tucked into the hutong is Beijing's first private restaurant, a couple of French cafés, and a scrappy clothing market.

Red Gate Gallery

Dongbianmen Watchtower, Chongwen; tel: 6525 1005; www.redgategallery.com; daily 10am–5pm; entrance fee (for the watchtower); subway: taxi from Jianguomen; map p.137 D3

This atmospheric gallery is housed in one of the rare chunks of the old city wall, the Ming Dynasty Dongbianmen Watchtower. It's one of the original art galleries and has a fine selection of contemporary art displayed in its creepy old rooms.

Tiananmen Square

Beijing Planning Exhibition Hall

20 Qianmen Dongdajie, Chongwen; tel: 6702 4559; Tue–Sun 9am–4pm; entrance fee; subway: Qianmen; map p.136 B3

For the best views of Beijing come here to see the city in miniature reproduction spread out over an entire floor as a scale model. Binoculars are available if you want a close up aerial view. The fourth-floor 3D theatre has some interesting videos of the city past and future. Unfortunately not much is in English.

Southern Beijing

Natural History Museum

126 Tianqiao Nandajie (near the Temple of Heaven west gate), Chongwen; tel: 6702 4431; Tue–Sun 8.30am–4pm; entrance fee; subway: taxi from Qianmen; map p.136 A1

This museum has thousands of stuffed animals and dinosaurs: in the centre of the main hall is the skeleton of the one-horned Qingdasaurus and visitors can race dinosaurs on a special test bicycle. The Hall of Human Bodies is tucked into a side building and is quite gruesome. There is a whole menagerie of stuffed animals and some rather funny robotic dinosaurs.

Gulou

Onemoon Gallery

Ditan Park (near the south gate entrance), Dongcheng; tel: 6427 7748; www.onemoonart.com; Tue–Sun 10am–6pm; subway: Jianguomen; map p.134 B4

Onemoon is an elegant gallery that is housed inside a beautifully-restored courtyard house. It shows a wide range of modern pieces, including a fair number of abstract works.

The Embassy District

C5 Art Centre

Building F, BITIC Building 5, Sanlitun 5 Jie, Chaoyang; tel: 6460 3950; www.c5art.com; daily 10am–7pm; subway: taxi from Dongzhimen; map p.135 E3

Right: animatronic dinosaur at the Beijing Museum of Natural History.

Left: the 798 district.

C5 is a funky new art gallery that concentrates on mixed media. It's located just north of the German Embassy.

Central Business District

Capital Museum

16 Fuxingmenwai Dajie, Xicheng; tel: 6337 0491; www.capitalmuseum.org.cn; Tue–Sun 9am–5pm; entrance fee; subway: Muxidi; map p.138 B4

While the National Museum of China is being essentially rebuilt, the Capital Museum is Beijing's main showpiece. The building is a peculiar mix of modern and ancient – there is a giant stone curtain wall that pierces the exterior, while inside it looks like a giant shopping centre with flights and flights of escalators. There are tens of thousands of exhibits including an interesting walk-through reconstruction of a hutong.

Western Beijing

Geological Museum of China

15 Yangrou Hutong, Xicheng; tel: 6655 7858; Tue–Sun 9am–4pm; entrance fee; subway: Fuchengmen; map p.133 D1

This hangar of a building hides a sparkling array of thousands of gems and crystals and explains, in fairly good English, geological phenomena including earthquakes, volcanoes and river erosion. Interactive exhibits allow you to design your own diamond and build a toy house and test whether it is quake-proof.

The North

Beijing Planetarium

138 Xizhimenwai Dajie; Xicheng; tel: 6835 2453; www.bjp.org.cn;

Right: traditional art on sale at Wan Fu Art Gallery.

Wed–Sun 9.30am–3.30pm; entrance fee; subway: Xizhimen; map p.132 B3

The newly-funked up planetarium spins visitors around the solar system and back in its daily space shows. It boasts an SGI digital space theatre with constellations beamed onto a cupola, a 3D spaceship simulator, and meteor fragments.

Beijing Science and Technology Museum

1 Beisanhuan Zhonglu, Chaoyang; tel: 6237 1177; Tue–Sun 9am–4.30pm; entrance fee; subway: taxi from Gulou

China doesn't miss a beat in promoting itself and the Science Museum is an ideal vehicle to show the world great Chinese inventions and recent scientific exploits– check out the Shenzhou Spaceship return capsule. That doesn't suck out all the fun, though, there are dozens of great exhibits including musical, kick-boxing robots and a Van de Graaf generator to give you a temporary Mohican.

Dashanzi, Factory 798

4 Jiuxianqiao Lu, Chaoyang; subway: taxi from Wangjing Xi

Dozens of galleries have been assembled in this East German-built complex of abandoned brick factory

buildings. Some of the plants are still working and occasionally belch out smoke creating a mysterious atmosphere. Some of the best galleries here are **Beijing Commune**, **Marella Gallery** and **White Space**.

77

Music, Dance and Theatre

Beijing prides itself as being a city of culture and after the opening of the striking new Chinese National Grand Theatre in late 2007 it now has a landmark venue to boot. For traditional performing arts, visitors from overseas delight in acrobatics, opera and kung fu – striking foreign theatre which blasts the senses. More familiar entertainment – western opera, classical and pop music and ballet – is performed by international names and some fine homegrown artists. Broadway musicals are also finding their way to Beijing.

Music

CLASSICAL

Beijing has two major orchestras – the **China National Symphony Orchestra** and the **China Philharmonic** – and more than half a dozen others that perform less regularly. It is also home to the **Central Conservatory of Music**, which was founded in the early 1950s at Zhou Enlai's behest, and is arguably the best conservatory in the country. The Beijing **International Music Festival** held every October has grown into a major international event with scores of top-notch performers from around the world.

Beijing Concert Hall
1 Beixinhua Jie, Xicheng; tel: 6605 7006; subway: Tiananmen West; map p.139 E4

The **Ancient Music Centre** in the Temple of Perfect Wisdom (Zhihuasi) on Lumicang Hutong (map p.135 D1) is a good place to catch Ming dynasty ritual music performances and Buddhist background music which is said to help monks memorize their chants

This hall will likely by overshadowed by the flashy National Grand Theatre, but it has good acoustics and hosts fine Chinese and western orchestras. Its main auditorium seats 1,000.

Forbidden City Concert Hall
Zhongshan Park, Xi Chang'an Jie, Dongcheng; tel: 6559 8285; subway: Tiananmen West; map p.136 A4

Boasts a magical location inside Zhongshan Park; the China Philharmonic are regular performers.

National Grand Theatre (National Centre for the Performing Arts)

Left and below right: traditional musicians at the Ancient Music Center.

2 Xichang'an Jie, Dongcheng; tel: 6655 0000; www.national grandtheatre.com; subway: Tiananmen West; map p.136 A4

The futuristic egg (see picture, p.80) sitting next to Tiananmen Square has three state-of-the art concert halls acoustically tuned for opera, orchestra and chamber music.

Poly Theatre
Poly Plaza, 14 Dongzhimen Nandajie; Dongcheng; tel: 6500 1188 ext. 5126; www.poly theatre.com; subway: Dongsishitiao; map p.135 D2

After the National Grand, the Poly Theatre has the best facilities for staging opera and concerts.

JAZZ

East Shore Live Jazz Café
Building 2, Qianhai Nanyan, Diananmenwai Dajie, Xicheng; tel: 8403 2131; subway: taxi from Gulou; map p.134 A2

Local jazz legend Liu Yuan opened this fabulous venue with panoramic views of

Left: the Midi Festival.

settle down to watch the show.

POP AND ROCK

Most big artists bypass Beijing altogether to please the crowds in Shanghai because the capital does not have a good-sized live music venue. **The Star Live** and **The Worker's Stadium** are the only two venues that come close enough to host globally-renowned acts. You can see rock, punk and pop bands at a sprinkling of live music venues listen below

2 Kolegas

21 Liangmaqiao Lu (inside the drive-in cinema complex), Chaoyang; tel: 8196 4820; www.2kolegas.com; subway: Liangmahe

A rough and ready music bar that plays dozens of bands and a lot of them local. Everything from ska to indie to punk, metal and rock. A bit of a trek out near the Fourth Ring Road.

D-22

13 Chengfu Lu, Haidian; tel: 6265 3177; subway: Wudaokou

Some local acts that are making it big are **Brain Failure** (punk), **Hedgehog** (pop), **Badboys Joyside** (punk), **Lonely China Day** (indie), **PK14** (currently the biggest name in Beijing rock) and **Snapline** (dance-rock).

Houhai Lake two years ago now. There's free live music every night, just make sure you get here before 9pm to get a seat.

Jianghu Live Show Bar

7 Dongmianhua Hutong (just off Nanluogu Xiang), Dongcheng; tel: 132 69227168; www.jianghu. bj.cn; subway: taxi from Zhangzizhonglu; map p.134 B2

Beijing's best kept little secret. This tiny courtyard dive has a small stage where local blues, jazz and folk bands play to an enthusiastic mainly local crowd.

Jiangjinjiu

2 Zhongku Hutong (between the Drum and Bell Towers), Dongcheng; tel: 8405 0124; subway: Gulou; map.134 A3

Good growly Mongolian folk and boisterous Xinjiang bands generally entertain in this jumbled hippy ethnic bar. You can order fresh Yunnan food, a beer, and

---

The good thing about listening to jazz in Beijing is that it's generally free. The premier venue is **East Shore Live** *(see p.78)* but there are several other establishments that lure with the saxophone. **Oriental Taipan Bar** (OT Lounge; 6 Ritan Lu; map p.137 D4) has jazz on Saturdays, **CD Jazz Café** (16 Dongsanhuan Beilu; map p.137 D4), which is growing a little stale but still has free shows daily, Japanese eatery **Jazz-Ya** (18 Sanlitun Beilu; map p.135 E3) has occasional live acts, and **Centro** (Kerry Centre; map p.137 E4) has an in-house jazz band.

Student grunge but hugely popular with Indie and rock fans. Drinks are cheap and nothing is wasted on the décor.

MAO Livehouse
111 Gulou Dongdajie, Dongcheng; tel: 133 6612 1459; subway: Baixinqiao; map p.134 B3
This black-painted warehouse space is a fabulous venue for live bands. Drinks are cheap, the crowd is local, and the sound system professional. More Brixton than West End.

Salud
66 Nanluogu Xiang, Dongcheng; tel: 6402 5086; subway: taxi from Gulou; map p.134 B3
A great little live music bar on Nanluogu Xiang. It's mostly guitar-strumming local expats that get the crowd swinging from the beams. Cheap drinks includ-

ing some sweet infused rums and an onsite bathroom make the French-owned Salud one of the most happening dives in the hood.

The Star Live
3rd Floor, Tango, 79 Hepingli Xijie (opposite the Lama Temple), Dongcheng; tel: 6425 5677; www.thestarlive.com; subway: Yonghegong; map p.134 C4
Despite the flashy VIP karaoke rooms below, this venue is good solid unpretentious venue for visiting bands.

What? Bar Forbidden City
72 Beichang Jie (near Forbidden City West Gate), Xicheng; tel: 139 1020 9249; subway: Tiananmen West; map p.134 A1
No bigger than a closet, this tiny bar hosts in-your-face punk and rock bands. It's been around for a fair few years and has a faithful following.

Yugong yishan
3–2 Zhangzi Zhonglu, Dongcheng; tel: 8402 8477; www.yugongyishan.com; subway: Zhangzizhong Lu; map p.134 B2
Yugong yishan has it all: a chilled rooftop bar, a great live set up with a decent sound system, some funky lasers, a generous-sized dance floor and super friendly staff. Their reper-

Beijing's biggest rock festival, the **Midi Festival**, usually takes place in May in Haidian Park. The event, which spans several days showcases good local bands as well as some well-known international acts. Another festival to look out for is the **Chaoyang Pop Music Festival**, a summertime slickly-run event which also attracts some big names in the pop and indie world.

toire includes rock, jazz, world, reggae, even good dance parties.

Dance

Beijing has several fine ballet and dance troupes including the **Central Ballet of China** and the **Beijing Modern Dance Company**. The best places to see dance performances are the **Beijing Exhibition Theatre** (see Theatre below), and **National Grand Theatre** (see p.78).

Theatre

Spoken drama enjoys an especially large and faithful audience in Beijing, whose people are known for their love of conversation. Most performances however are inaccessible to foreign audiences because they will be in

You can easily buy theatre and stage tickets from a number of English-language websites. You can pay with cash on delivery or via the Internet with a credit card. Delivery is free within the Fourth Ring Road, but total usually has to be over RMB100 or RMB200. See www.emma.cn (tel: 400 707 9999) or www.piao.com.cn (tel: 6417 7845).

Above, left and below right: acrobats at the Chaoyang Theatre.

Chinese. The **Poly Theatre** *(see p.78)*, the **National Grand Theatre** *(see p.78)* and the **Beijing Exhibition Theatre** will be the most likely places to see international performances in English, and increasingly, Broadway musicals (*Cats* slinked here in January 2008).

Beijing Exhibition Theatre
135 Xizhimenwai Dajie, Xicheng; tel: 6835 4455; subway: Xizhimen; map p.132 C3
Hosts an eclectic range of performances from Mongolian Folk Dancing to full-on chorus line Broadway musicals.

Acrobatics

Acrobatics are a traditional form of street theatre in

China and are also an important element in Beijing Opera and in many Chinese martial arts. Most regular acrobatics shows in Beijing are performed by young students, usually including children.

Chaoyang Theatre
36 Dongsanhuan Beilu, Chaoyang; tel: 6507 2421; www.acrobatics.com.cn; subway: taxi from Guomao; map p.135 E1
Chaoyang Theatre is the flashiest of the three main acrobatics theatres with laser shows and smoke machines to puff up all the juggling, leaping and contortions.

Tianqiao Acrobatic Theatre
95 Tianqiao Shichang Lu, Xuanwu; tel: 6303 7449; subway: taxi from Qianmen; map p.136 A1
This old theatre is home to less tourist acrobatic renditions; a lot of the performers are very young students.

Universal Theatre (Heaven and Earth, *Tiandi*)
10 Dongzhimen Nandaijie, Dongcheng; tel: 6416 9893; subway: Dongsishitiao; map p.135 D2
The China Acrobatic Troupe performs nightly here. Some

say its brand of professionalism make this the capital's best place to see traditional acrobatics.

Kung Fu

Chinese opera traditionally has had a kung fu element, but the martial arts extravaganzas put on in Beijing are firmly for the delight of overseas visitors.

The Red Theatre
44 Xingfu Dajie; Chongwen; tel: 6714 2473; www.legendof kungfu.com; subway: taxi from Tiantan Dongmen; map p.137 C2
Swirling monks, bubbles, aerial ballet and crashing music. If you want a spectacle the Legend of Kung Fu makes plenty, every night.

Left: the National Grand Theatre.

81

Nightlife

For some years now Beijing has been slowly becoming one of the funky new venues for major international DJ's and a slew of homegrown turntable talent. Money has been pumped into pimping out the city's nightlife and while some of it is more flash than funk, the clubbing scene is now both varied and vibrant. The previous heavy emphasis on hip hop been diluted with some great electronica nights. For information on Gay and Lesbian venues *see p.57*; for information on pop, rock and jazz concerts *see Music, Dance and Theatre, p.78–80*

Main Clubbing Districts

While there are a few core areas where the clubs coagulate, some of the best venues are snuck down their own secret little hutong. The natural lifespan of a Beijing club, like that of the capital's new bars and restaurants, is notoriously short-lived. Competition is fierce and patrons are fickle. For that reason, the majority of venues listed below have proved their stripes by lasting at least 12 months.

Gongti Xilu has a strip of neon behemoths and attracts the local nouveau riches whose drink of choice is the inexplicable green tea and Chivas – for evidence of the fat wallets in town check out the BMW's and Mercedes in the car park. **Gongti** itself boasts four or five thumping clubs inside its walls, while just east is the scruffier **Sanli-tun bar district**. Sanlitun has a couple of smaller funky clubs but the main queue of copycat bars, popular with less affluent locals, and with cover bands is not much fun. Further east again, is **Chaoyang Gongyuan Ximen**

(West Gate of Chaoyang Park). Outside of the outrageously ostentatious **Block 8** entertainment complex housing the glam **i-Ultra Lounge** and there are some hip and less pricey dance joints which attract a young mixed crowd of locals and expatriates. The free listings magazines, *That's Beijing* and *City Weekend* both carry clubs and events listings.

Clubs

The megaclubs popular with locals are often criticised for having all the wrong priorities – their patrons are more concerned with being seen than about getting good music. And so to this end, décor is bling-heavy, think crystals and flashing lights, and bar tables for posing encroach upon valuable dance floor space. The smaller bar-clubs are often more tastefully designed and play better music. Almost all clubs charge a small fee (RMB30–50) during the weekend; more if a big name is playing.

Famous name DJ's usually play one of the **Banana** joints *(see p.83)* because the brand has nabbed some serious pulling power with a deal for Chivas sponsorship.

Some of the heavyweights who have played recently in Beijing are Carl Cox, Paul Oakenfold, Paul Van Dyk and Goldie; while some local DJ's to look out for are Patrick Yu (drum'n'bass), Mickey Zhang (techno) and Yang Bing

With last trains leaving around 11pm anyway, getting home late at night usually means resorting to a cab. There is no shortage of taxis in the early hours of the morning and drivers collect around the bigger clubs in anticipation of a ride. Remember to bring your hotel card.

Left: Suzy Wong's.

attracts the big names on the decks. The club, though, has a tiny dance floor, an ear-drum shattering sound system, poor service, and gets insufferably crowded on weekends.

Mix

Gongren Tiyuchan Beimen (inside Worker's Stadium North Gate), Chaoyang; tel: 6530 2889; subway: Gongti Beilu; map p.135 D2

Beijing's single most successful club is packed every night of the week and attracts a faithful following of hip hop fans. A good place to people watch Beijing's new clubbing generation.

Remix

Gongren Tiyuchan Beimen (inside Worker's Stadium North Gate), Chaoyang; tel: 6530 2889; subway: Gongti Beilu; map p.135 D2

One of Beijing's newest clubs, Remix's big boast is its function one sound system, supposedly besting that of all other clubs in the capital. Despite the over-the-top décor it has a decent-sized dance floor and sound-enhancing padded walls.

White Rabbit

C2 Haoyunjie (Lucky Street), 29 Zaoying Lu, Maizidian, Chaoyang; tel: 133 2112 3678; subway: Maizidian Xilu

A bit far out in Lucky Street, east of the Third Ring Road, but worth it if you are a serious clubber. Its Berlin-club inspired greyness allows the venue to concentrate on playing good music. Usually gets kicking after midnight.

The World of Suzy Wong

Chaoyang Gonyuan Xilu, Chaoyang; tel: 6595 5049; subway: Gongti Beilu

Enormously popular cocktail bar, dance club and pick-up joint, Suzy Wong's is now a Beijing institution. Best in summer when the rooftop terrace is open.

With all the bewildering amount of new construction work, several upscale venues, including rumours of a good crop of members' clubs, promise to outdo themselves in efforts to score big on the luxurious scale. Spots to look out for include the **Legation Club** near Tiananmen Square and **1949, the Hidden City** just off Nansanlitun Lu. It promises to be a swish club and restaurant complex in the style of olde Beijing.

(techno). Yen Club, Acupuncture Records and The Syndicate (drum'n'bass) are three local outfits that hold occasional and very popular rave-style parties.

Banana GT

Scitech Hotel, 22 Jianguomenwai Dajie, Chaoyang; tel: 6528 3636; subway: Jianguomen; map p.137 D4

Newly renovated, this mega-club has proved its staying power: it is one of the original Beijing clubs. Banana has a sunken dance floor and an erotically-inspired choreograph regime of scantily clad men and women suspended in cages. Attracts a fairly local crowd and gets packed out when international acts play.

China Doll

2/F Tongli, Sanlitun, Chaoyang; tel: 6417 4699; subway: Gongti Beilu; map p.135 E3

China Doll is a slick dance club and bar spread over three floors. The sub-aquatic design is particularly stylish – walls are hung with photos of beautiful semi-naked women cavorting underwater.

Club Obiwan

Xihai, 4 Xiyan, Xicheng; tel: 6617 3231; subway: Jishuitan; map p.135 E4

This tumbledown and friendly club is hidden down a lakeside hutong just south of Jishuitan subway. Strictly non-pretentious and beers are cheap. It has an eclectic dance floor policy – reggae Sundays; house, indie and 80's the rest of the time. Great roof garden with views of Xihai Lake.

CocoBanana

6 Gongren Tiyuchan Xilu, Chaoyang; tel: 8599 9999; subway: Gongti Beilu; map p.135 D2

Smaller sister to Banana, this very popular haunt regularly

The Olympics

It was one of modern China's proudest moments when in 2001, the International Olympic Committee announced Beijing had won the bid to host the 2008 Games. The city has embraced its Olympic slogan, 'One World, One Dream' with the Games acting like a giant catalyst, throwing it into top gear to get ready for the big event. Construction has been madcap: everything from avant-garde stadiums to kilometres of new subway lines have been built. The proof, ultimately, is in the pudding. The number 8 is considered lucky by the Chinese, so it all kicks off at the auspicious time and date of 8 August 2008, at 8.08pm.

Getting Accommodation

By now the 220,000 or so rooms in Beijing's hotels and guesthouses are fully booked for the Olympics and have waiting lists as long as the Great Wall. They will be raking it in: establishments are asking for 15-day minimum stays and have upped rates about 400 percent. A room in a five-star hotel, if you can get one, is going for around $1,000 a night. Perhaps the only choice left is to rent an apartment for the two weeks or opt for a homestay. The government is running a program via www.beijingroommate.com/homestay2008.htm; they expect to be fully booked by end-March but they may launch an extension. For US$900 for a month, they offer a room in a host family house, one meal a day, with one family member able to speak English and a free airport pick-up. For other homestay options try www.tour-beijing.com/beijing_homestay, www.olympic-booking.com/Homestay.htm or www.meetinbeijing2008.com. To rent an apartment from a private

Above: the mascots for 2008.

landlord or an enterprising expatriate – expect to get charged royally – try www.homestaybeijing2008.com. As an example of the price gouging, a two-bedroom courtyard house in Dongsishitiao is going for RMB7,500 a night for a minimum 20 nights stay.

The Venues

Some 31 of the Olympic venues are in Beijing and a good proportion of them are clustered around the Olympic Village in the north of the city. The centrepiece is the 91,000 seat **National Stadium** nicknamed the **Bird's Nest** for its steel latticework which cups the exterior. The opening and closing ceremonies and the core athletics events will be

held here. After the Olympics, the stadium will be used for sports events and rock concerts. Next door is the equally loopy 17,000-seater **National Aquatics Centre** or **Water Cube** which looks like a giant mattress. At night the soap-bubble-like walls glow blue. During the day they allow natural light to heat up the pools inside conserving energy. When the Games are over the building can be reassembled to make a smaller leisure centre and a shopping centre.

Getting to the venues should be easy. A 4.4-km (2.7 mile) Olympics subway spur line will be tested in June and

Right: clean-air measures have been taken to protect athletes.

Left: the Bird's Nest, under consruction.

region of Tibet, also seems to be lost on the organisers.

Human Rights

Western rights groups and media have been keenly laying into China in the run up to the Games, slaying it for everything from its poor human rights record to its unmanageable pollution. Reports document dodgy air quality records, crackdowns in Tibet, on journalists and writers and even an alleged cover up over deaths of construction workers building Olympic stadiums – at least 10 are alleged to have died building the National Stadium. Beijing is defensive about these allegations while tightening controls on dissent in the background is doing its best to present an open and friendly front to the world. In February 2008, when US director Stephen Spielberg quit as artistic advisor for the Olympics over China's role in propping up the Sudanese government – Beijing buys its oil and sells it weapons – the Chinese reacted angrily, said it was wrong to politicise the Olympics. Unfortunately for them, this proved only the beginning of the games' politicisation: Tibetan protesters met the Olympic torch at nearly every leg of its relay.

The official website of the 2008 Beijing Olympic Games is at http://en.beijing2008.cn.

---

be up and running by the time of the Games. It will link the city with all the main Olympic venues. Fares will be a flat rate RMB2.
SEE ALSO ARCHITECTURE, P.31

The Mascots

It is an unwritten rule in this world that Olympic mascots must be mocked. And Beijing's creations, while certainly cute, have not been immune to the scorn. The five chubby *fuwa* (lucky dolls), are modelled on four animals – the fish, the Tibetan antelope, the panda and the swallow, and – ahem – a fire. Each one corresponds to an Olympic ring colour – the panda skirted the black and white problem by going with green (bamboo leaves were stuffed behind its ears). The cheeky characters look suspiciously like furry power puff girls, and each one is a clone of the other – the fish and the fire, for example, differ only in their hue and their hairstyle – the fish has a dodgy perm while the fire's crown is ringed by licks of flame. The irony of using the antelope, an animal from the disputed

The uber-luxurious **Beijing Seven Star Morgan Plaza** will be perched overlooking the National Stadium. The extra two stars it has awarded itself are for its intensive butler service – three staff members for each of its 270 rooms. Media reports have it that Bill Gates has booked a penthouse for the Games.

Palaces and Homes

It is the pomp and circumstance of imperial Beijing that so fascinates visitors. The Forbidden City functioned as the fulcrum of the ordered cosmos that was imperial China, the hallowed nucleus of the empire for nearly five centuries. More playful are the Summer Palaces, great landscaped gardens and lavish halls built outside Beijing for the pleasure of the emperor and his court. Now these hallowed places are open to all, and thanks to the Olympics, have undergone major restoration work.

Along Chang'an Jie

The Forbidden City
Chang'an Jie, Dongcheng; tel: 8511 7311; daily, winter: 8.30am–4.30pm, summer: 8.30am–5pm; entrance fee; subway: either of the Tiananmen stations; map p.136 A1
Try to get to this great palace complex, also known as the Imperial Palace (*Gugong* in pinyin), early in the day – it will take a good couple of hours to get

through – and buy an all-inclusive ticket, as some of the halls have exhibitions which otherwise require separate tickets.

Within its thick red ramparts a succession of emperors lived and ruled, aided and served by tens of thousands of officials, eunuchs, maids and concubines. The eunuchs were employees for life, and their mincing footsteps, high

The Forbidden City is sometimes jokingly referred to as the 'place with 9,999½ rooms', as only Heaven has 10,000. (In fact it has 8,706 rooms and halls.)

voices and – some said – scent of urine were a fixture of palace life. So, too, were the concubines, highly educated young women forever cut off from their families and the world outside, fated to spend their days sewing – and, perhaps, conniving – as they awaited the emperor's pleasure.

The Forbidden City is divided into two main areas – the southern (front) section or Outer Courtyard, comprising three large halls, in which the Ming and Qing emperors held state ceremonies, and the residential northern (rear) section or Inner Courtyard, consisting of three large palaces and a few smaller ones, and the Imperial Gardens.

Left: street artists create and sell their work at the Forbidden City.

Left: looking over the Forbidden City.

HALLS IN HARMONY

There are three large audience and throne halls at the end of this courtyard that stand on a marble platform more than 8m (26ft) high and divided into three levels. The balustrades on each level are decorated with dragon heads that spout water when it rains.

The **Hall of Supreme Harmony** *(Taihedian)* is the largest of the three halls. Within the hall stood the **Dragon Throne**, from where the emperor ruled. The roof of the hall is supported by 72 pillars, with the inner six adorned by dragons. It has the most imposing roof in the palace, with a horizontal ridge, four roof-trees and double eaves. Its dragons, at a weight of 4.5 tonnes and a height of 3m (10ft), are the largest in the palace. Altogether, there are the figures of 10 animals on the roof, and one immortal, to serve as protection against evil spirits.

In the smallest of the three halls, the **Hall of**

THE OUTER COURTYARD

The massive bulk of the **Meridian Gate** *(Wumen)* is the entrance to the Forbidden City. At 38m (125ft) it is the tallest gate of the palace. From a throne in the middle pavilion of the gate the emperor reviewed military parades, announced new calendars, and ordered rebellious officials to be punished.

Once inside the Meridian Gate you enter a large courtyard, bisected by the **Golden Water River** *(Jinshahe)* and crossed by five marble bridges. Across this first courtyard to the north is the **Gate of Supreme Harmony** *(Taihemen)*, rebuilt in 1890. Inside it there is a large map of the palace. Beyond this gate is the largest courtyard in the complex, the **Court of the Imperial Palace**, where the imperial shops selling silk and porcelain were situated.

Sacred Geometry

Its architecture raised the Forbidden City above all earthly things. Huge red walls enclosed the inner sanctum, an area forbidden to ordinary mortals. No building in the rest of Beijing was permitted to be taller than the walls of the palace. The buildings were aligned on north–south lines, the most important of them orientated to face south. Many of them have names based on Confucian philosophy – endless combinations of 'harmony', 'peace' and 'quiet' – which were considered to have lucky connotations.

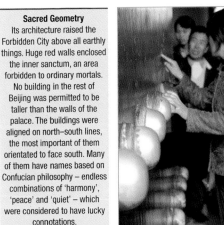

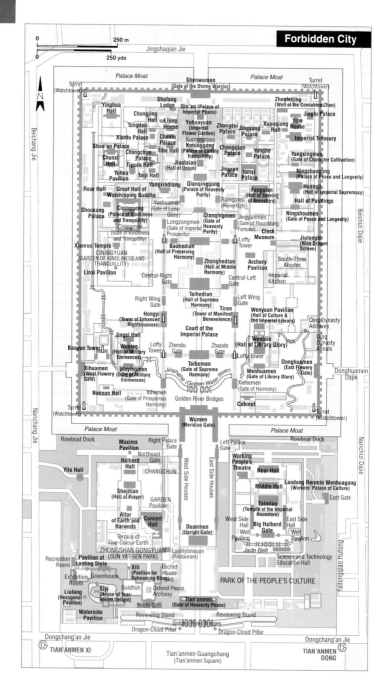

Forbidden City

0 — 250 m
0 — 250 yds

Jingshaqian Jie

Palace Moat

Palace Moat

Turret (Watchtower)

Turret (Watchtower)

Shenwumen (Gate of the Divine Warrior)

Zhenfeijing (Well of the Concubine Zhen)

Jingfu Palace

Shufang Lodge

Qin'an (Palace of Imperial Peace)

Yinghua Hall

Chongjing Hall

Lijing House

Yuhuayuan (Imperial Flower Garden)

Zhongcui Palace

Jingyang Palace

Xuanqiong Hall

Ylhe House

Tongdao Hall

Imperial Treasury

Xianfu Palace

Chuxiu Palace

Kunningmen

Chengqian Palace

Yonghe Palace

Yangxingmen (Gate of Character Cultivation)

Shou'an Palace

The Hall

Kuningong (Palace of Earthly Tranquility)

Changchun Palace

Jiaotaian (Hall of Union)

Jingren Palace

Yanxi Palace

Ningshougong (Palace of Peace and Longevity)

Chunxi Hall

Tiyuan Hall

Yuhua Pavilion

Taiji Hall

Yangxindian

Qianqinggong (Palace of Heavenly Purity)

Fengxian (Hall of Serving of Ancestors)

Huangji (Hall of Imperial Supremacy)

Rear Hall

Great Hall of Worshipping Buddha

Rujingmen (Rijing Gate)

Hall of Paintings

Ciningong (Palace of Kindliness and Tranquility)

Yuehuamen (Gate of Lunar Glory)

Qianqingmen (Gate of Heavenly Purity)

Jingyunmen (Gate of Flourishing Fortune)

Ningshoumen (Gate of Peace and Longevity)

Shoukang Palace

Ciningmen (Gate of Kindliness and Tranquility)

Longzongmen (Gate of Imperial Prosperity)

Clock Museum

Xianrud Temple

CININGYUAN (GARDEN OF KINDLINESS AND TRANQUILLITY)

Baohedian (Hall of Preserving Harmony)

Lofty Tower

Jiulongbi (Nine Dragon Screen)

Linxi Pavilion

Central-Right Gate

Zhonghedian (Hall of Middle Harmony)

Archery Pavilion

South-Three Abodes

Central-Left Gate

Imperial Kitchen

Taihedian (Hall of Supreme Harmony)

Right Wing Gate

Left Wing Gate

Tiren (Tower of Manifest Benevolence)

Wenyuan Pavilion (Hall of Culture & Old Imperial Library)

Qing-Dynasty Archives

Hongyi (Tower of Enhanced Righteousness)

Court of the Imperial Palace

Jingsi Hall

Lofty Tower

Zhendu Gate

Zhaode Gate

Wenhua (Hall of Library Glory)

Lofty Tower

Donghuamen (East Flowery Gate)

Qing Dynasty Annals

Baoyun Tower

Wuying (Hall of Military Eminences)

Wuyingmen (Gate of Military Eminences)

Taihemen (Gate of Supreme Harmony)

Wenhuamen (Gate of Library Glory)

Xiehemen (Gate of Harmony)

Xihuamen (West Flowery Gate)

Jinshuihe (Golden Water River)

Donghuamen Dajie

Nanxun Hall

Xihemen (Gate of Prosperous Harmony)

Golden River Bridges

Cabinet

Turret (Watchtower)

Turret (Watchtower)

Wumen (Meridian Gate)

Palace Moat

Palace Moat

Rowboat Dock

Maxims Pavilion

Right Palace Gate

Left Palace Gate

Rowboat Dock

Yile Hall

Northeast Gate

Halberd Hall

West Side Houses

East Side Houses

Working People's Theatre

Rear Hall

Laodong Renmin Wenhuagong (Workers' Palace of Culture)

CHANGCHUN

Shejitian (Hall of Prayer)

GARDEN Pavilion

Middle Hall

East Gate

Altar of Earth and Harvests

Concert Hall

Taimiao (Temple of the Imperial Ancestors)

West Side Hall

Big Halberd Gate

East Side Hall

Terrace of Five-Colour Earth

Duanmen (Upright Gate)

Well Pavilion

Jade Belt

Well Pavilion

Recreation Room

Pavilion of Lanting Stele

Laijinyunxuan (Restaurant)

Science and Technology Education Hall

Xili (Pavilion for Rehearsing Rites)

House Gate

PARK OF THE PEOPLE'S CULTURE

Exhibition Room

Greenhouse

Goldfish

Defend Peace Archway

Feilongqiao Hutong

Liufang (Hexagonal Pavilion)

Siyi (House of Year Round Delight)

Waterside Pavilion

South Gate

Tian'anmen (Gate of Heavenly Peace)

Reviewing Stand

Reviewing Stand

Golden Water Bridges

Dragon-Cloud Pillar

Dragon-Cloud Pillar

Dongchang'an Jie

Dongchang'an Jie

TIAN'ANMEN XI

Tian'anmen Guangchang (Tian'anmen Square)

TIAN'ANMEN DONG

Beichang Jie

Nanchang Jie

Beichzi Dajie

Nanchzi Dajie

ZHONGSHAN GONGYUAN (SUN YAT-SEN PARK)

Middle Harmony *(Zhonghedian)*, the emperor prepared for ceremonies before entering the main hall. There is an imperial palanquin on display here. The last of the three great halls, the **Hall of Preserving Harmony** *(Baohedian)*, was used in the lavish New Year's banquets, as well as for examinations.

THE REAR COURTYARDS

The northern section of the Imperial Palace is entered through the **Gate of Heavenly Purity** *(Qianqingmen)*, which leads to three large palaces: the **Palace of Heavenly Purity**, the **Hall of Union** and the **Palace of Earthly Tranquillity**. These palaces were the living and working quarters of the Ming and Qing emperors, and the scene of plots and intrigues between eunuchs and concubines in their manoeuvrings for power and influence within the court.

The **Palace of Heavenly Purity** *(Qianqinggong)* was the bedroom of the Ming emperors, but later in the Qing dynasty it was used for audiences with officials and foreign envoys. The successor to the imperial throne was announced from here. Immediately to the north is the **Hall of Union** *(Jiaotaian)*,

The male palace servants were without exception eunuchs, therefore ensuring that after dark the emperor would be the only male capable of begetting a new generation. For many Chinese, especially for the poor, it was lucrative to enter the imperial service as a eunuch. Surgeons, called 'knifers', stationed themselves at the gates to the Forbidden City. Here, they would perform castrations at 'reasonable rates', but then sell the sexual organs back to the victims at a high price, for the organs had to be presented in a bottle for inspection at the palace.

Above: the bridges over the Golden Water River.

where imperial concubines were officially approved. Within the hall are the imperial jade seals as well as a water-clock dating back to 1745. The third palace, to the rear, is the **Palace of Earthly Tranquillity** *(Kuninggong)*, the residence of the Ming empresses.

To the sides of the Palace of Heavenly Purity lie the East and West Palaces, grouped like the constellations around the pole star. Here, the emperor was the only mature adult male, surrounded by concubines, eunuchs, the empress, serving women and slaves. As late as 1900, there were still 10,000 people living in the palace.

DRAGONS AND LONGEVITY

To the southeast is the **Nine Dragon Screen** *(Jiulongbi)*, built out of brightly coloured glazed bricks. The dragon is a symbol of Heaven and, therefore, of the emperor, as is the number nine, the highest unit.

Left: Buddhist monks visiting the Forbidden City.

Nearby there is a fascinating **Clock Museum**, filled with a spectacular array of timepieces collected by Qing emperors. Opposite the Nine Dragon Screen is the **Gate of Peace and Longevity** *(Ningshoumen)*, which leads to the **Palace of Peace and Longevity** *(Ningshougong)*. The 18th-century emperor Qianlong had this complex built for his old age. The **Imperial Treasury** is now housed in the adjoining halls to the north. On display are golden cutlery and table silver, jewellery, robes, porcelain, cloisonné, hunting equipment and golden religious objects.

THE NORTHERN EXIT

Follow the red palace walls to the west. Before leaving the palace it's worth taking time to see the **Imperial Flower Garden** *(Yuhuayuan)*. Laid out during the Ming period, it exemplifies the traditional Chinese skill at landscape gardening. Leave the Imperial Palace by way of the **Gate of the Divine Warrior** *(Shenwumen)*.

Left: architectural details from the Forbidden City.

treated to a sample of Beijing Opera.

SEE ALSO BEIJING OPERA, P.35

Soong Qingling's Former Residence

46 Houhai Beiyan, Dongcheng; tel: 6404 4205 ext. 815; daily 9am–4pm; entrance fee; subway: Gulou; map p.134 A3

The former home of Song Qingling, honorary president of the People's Republic of China, and wife of Sun Yatsen, is a few doors down from Prince Gong's. The grounds were formerly part of the palace of Prince Chun, Pu Yi's father. The house where Pu Yi was born is just south of here.

Song Qingling moved into the house in 1963 and lived there until her death in 1981. The guest room contains an exhibition of photographs, documents and objects from her life: her pampered Shanghai childhood as a daughter of one of China's most prominent families, her years as a student, her marriage to Sun Yat-sen, and her political activities and support for the resistance to Japanese occupation. An extract from her most famous speech, the essay 'Sun Yatsen and his Cooperation with the Communist Party', is also on display.

The Lake District

Guo Moruo's Former Residence

18 Qianhai Xijie, Xicheng; tel: 6612 5392; Tue–Sun 9am–4.30pm; entrance fee; subway: taxi from Zhangzizhonglu; map p.134 A2

Guo Moruo, an influential figure in the rise of Communism in China, was born in Sichuan Province in 1892, the son of a wealthy landlord. He became known as a respected author as well as a proponent of change and an early adherent of the fledgling Chinese Communist Party, meeting with Mao in 1926. He later held several posts in the new Communist state. Guo was one of the first people to be attacked by the Red Guards during the Cultural Revolution. The buildings are set in leafy grounds; inside, among the polished floors and old furniture, are photographs and quotations from the great man, but most are captioned in Chinese only.

Palace of Prince Gong (Gong Wang Fu)

14a Liuyin Jie (near the west bank of Houhai), Dongcheng; tel: 6616 8149; daily 8.30am–4.30pm; entrance fee; subway: Gulou; map p.133 E3

This is the world's largest extant courtyard house. Prince Gong, the brother of Emperor Xian Feng, virtually ran the country from 1861 to 1884. The historic structures in the complex include Beijing's only preserved Qingdynasty theatre. Here, guests are served by women wearing traditional costumes of the period and

Western Fringes

The New Summer Palace (Yiheyuan)

Yiheyuan Lu, Haidian; tel: 6288 1144; daily, winter 7am–5pm,

If you want to travel to the Summer Palace as Cixi did, you can float along the canal. Craft leave from Yuyuantan Park near the CCTV Tower in the west at 9.30am and noon in the summer (tel: 6852 9428).

---

summer 7am–6pm; entrance fee; subway: taxi from Wudaokou; map p.24
This mosaic of imperial pleasure gardens and grand buildings, harmoniously arranged on hills around a beautiful lake, was partially destroyed in 1900 but quickly rebuilt – and has since survived civil war and the Cultural Revolution to become one of Beijing's top attractions, visited by hundreds of thousands every year.

Beautiful **Kunming Lake** covers about two-thirds of the area of the *Yiheyuan* complex, adding a sense of serenity and silence. In summer, the lake is covered with a carpet of huge, round, green lotus leaves, while pale-pink lotus flowers rise between them.

The great artificial hill, 60m (197ft) in height, which rises behind the palace was named

Above: the Marble Boat.

Longevity Hill (Wanshoushan) by Qianlong, in honour of his mother on her 60th birthday.

The main path into the grounds leads through a mighty wooden *pailou*, a kind of Chinese triumphal arch, past the ghost wall that is supposed to ward off all evil influences, directly to the

Eastern Gate (*Donggong-men*). Visible beyond this is the **Hall of Benevolence and Longevity** (*Renshoudian*), with its opulent furnishings and decorative objets d'art. This is where young Emperor Guangxu dealt with state business when the imperial court resided in *Yiheyuan*.

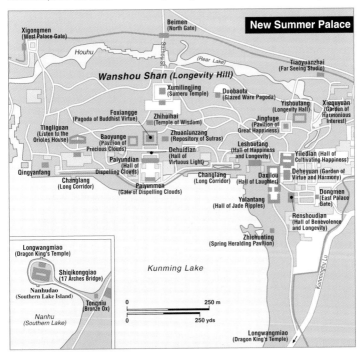

91

P

It was in the nearby **Hall of Jade Ripples** *(Yulantang)* that Empress Dowager Cixi supposedly kept Guangxu under house arrest for his folly at attempting to reform a crumbling dynasty by opening China to foreign ideas in 1898.

Not far from the Hall of Jade Ripples, on the southeastern slopes of Longevity Hill, were Cixi's private living and sleeping apartments, the **Hall of Happiness and Longevity** *(Leshoutang)*. Served by a staff of 48, she did not want for much except privacy.

Cixi was passionate about Beijing Opera. She had an impressive open-air stage built in the **Garden of Virtue and Harmony** *(Deheyuan)*. Its three stages, one above the other, were connected by trapdoors, so that supernatu-

ral beings, saints and immortals could swoop down into the operatic scene and evil spirits could rise from the depths of the underworld. There was even an underground water reservoir for 'wet' scenes. Today, it is a theatre museum.

A highlight in the further eastern part of the palace gardens is the **Garden of Harmonious Interest** *(Xiequyuan)*, a complete, perfect and beautiful replica of a lotus pool from the Wuxi area in Central China.

The **Long Corridor** *(Changlang)* is 728m (2,388ft) in length and runs along the foot of the hill parallel to the shore of Kunming Lake. The ceilings and rafters of the walkway are decorated with countless bird-and-flower motifs.

In the middle of the walkway, where the east–west axis of the palace park meets the north–south axis, the **Gate of Dispelling Clouds** *(Paiyunmen)* – a great triumphal arch – marks the start of the climb up **Longevity Hill**. Next to 12 massive, bizarre-shaped stones symbolising the signs of the Chinese zodiac, is an elegant pair of lions cast in bronze – perhaps the most beautiful in all of Beijing – guarding an imposing Buddhist temple complex, which is surrounded by a red wall. Go through two gates and over a bridge to reach the **Hall of Dispelling Clouds** *(Paiyundian)*.

The massive, 38m (125 ft) tall, octagonal **Pagoda of Buddhist Virtue** *(Foxiangge)* is up a steep staircase. This is the highest point of the palace, and from here is a wonderful panoramic view.

To the east is a group of buildings, the **Repository of Sutras** *(Zhuanlunzang)*, once used as the archives for copies of Confucian classics and Buddhist scrolls. To the west is a rare

The ruins of *Yuanmingyuan* remain a powerful symbol of China's humiliation at the hands of the West. The memory of its destruction is regularly evoked as a reminder of the dangers of both Western imperialism and domestic political and military weakness. Indeed, the large sign just outside the eastern gate of the ruins greets visitors with the words, 'Do not forget the national shame, rebuild the Chinese nation.'

Above: virtue, present and past.

and quite extraordinary masterpiece of Chinese architecture – the **Pavilion of Precious Clouds** (*Baoyunge*), framed on all four sides by smaller pavilions and walkways. Its stepped roof and its beams, columns and struts make it look like a wooden building, yet they were all cast from bronze in 1750 with the help of wax moulds.

A little further to the west, at the end of the Long Corridor lies the famous **Marble Boat** (*Qingyanfang*), with its two stone wheels on either side. Cixi is thought to have squandered a fortune on this spectacular folly, money that should have gone to the Chinese navy – with the

direct result a humiliating naval defeat by the Japanese in 1895.

The Old Summer Palace (Yuanmingyuan)
28 Qinghua Xilu, Haidian; tel: 6262 8501; daily, winter: 7am–5pm, summer: 7am–6.30pm; entrance fee; subway: taxi from Wudaokou; map p.24

The magnificent complex of park and palace that once stood here was the creation of Emperor Qianlong. He called it *Yuanmingyuan*: the Garden of Perfect Purity. Little remains of the original Summer Palace, although its large grounds are now a park

providing a quiet retreat from the city, and are a popular place for weekend picnics. The main entrance is at the southern end of the complex. Inside, a web of paths make their way through the park. The rebuilt maze is particularly fun. Past a wide depression in the terrain is a broad field of ruins, where the remains of ornate pillars and frescos are more reminiscent of European Baroque buildings than the architecture of imperial China. During the Second Opium War, Lord Elgin, the commander-in-chief of the British forces, ordered the destruction of *Yuanmingyuan*.

Modern Beijingers come here especially to enjoy **Fu Hai Lake**. In the summer, hundreds of paddle and rowing boats bob in the water and, in the winter, skaters glide over the ice. Also popular is the eastern section, the **Eternal Spring Garden** (*Changchunyuan*), with the European fountain ruins – one of the more intact structures in the complex.

Left: Kunming Lake, New Summer Palace.

Pampering

Steam baths and hot springs were popular with the noble classes as early as the Han dynasty 2,200 years ago. These days Beijing's growing affluence has also meant the rocket-like growth of high-end spas. Glossy bilingual monthlies, such as *Spa China*, chart their rise. Now you can get oiled, rubbed, scrubbed, sloughed and kneaded like the best of them at exclusive luxury resorts and five-star hotels as well as at cheaper locally run massage parlours and beauticians. See *Chinese Medicine, p.40–1* for information on where to go for a traditional Chinese massage.

Day Spas

Bodhi
2/F, 17 Gongren Tiyuchan Beilu, Chaoyang; tel: 6417 9595; daily 11am–midnight; subway: Gongti Beilu; map p.135 E2
Small and simple, Bodhi has a chilled atmosphere and gives pleasant massages. Free snacks and juice come with each treatment. They also offer a wide range of styles for such a small establishment, including Ayurvedic and a Thai herbal treatment.

Dragonfly
60 Donghuamen Dajie (near the Forbidden City), Dongcheng;

tel: 6527 9369; daily 11am–1am; www.dragonfly.net.cn; subway: Tiananmen East; map p.136 B4
Dragonfly is a chain that has several branches around Beijing and in Shanghai. A nice ambience is created by candles and subtle lighting, and prices are about a quarter of those charged in hotel spas for, some say, pretty much the same experience. Dragonfly offers Chinese, aromatherapy oil, foot, and Japanese Shiatsu massages, including hangover treatmentsr. Facials, manicures and waxing (even playboy) are on the menu.

Huaxi Aloe
17 Kuanjie (Zhangzi Zhonglu), Dongcheng; tel: 6405 2888; daily 9am–9pm; subway: Zhangzizhonglu; map p.134 B2
Aloe is at play here, a gooey, sticky green gel that is supposed to have relaxing and beautifying properties. You can opt for an hour of the gloop on your face or bathe in the stuff. Staff do not speak great English, but prices are low (bargain), and whatever magical properties it may or may not have, an aloe treatment is about the most refreshing thing you can do in dusty Beijing.

I Spa
5/F, Tower 2, Taiyue Suites, 16 Nansanlitun Lu, Chaoyang; tel: 6507 1517; daily 11am–11pm; subway: Gongti Beilu; map p.135 E2
I Spa is a slickly run, super-popular Thai spa that has Thai masseuses and is a great mid-range option. They offer about a dozen different services, including a jasmine rice body scrub, a green tea body wrap and a massage

Left: hot stone massage.

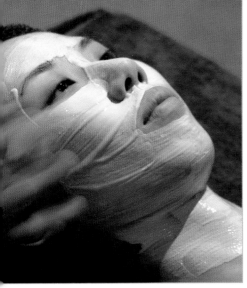

Left: a facial at CHI.

CHI
Shangri-La Hotel, 29 Zizhuyuan Lu, Haidian; tel: 6841 2211; daily 10am–11pm; subway: taxi from Xizhimen; map p.132 A3
CHI is Beijing's most beautiful spa, with the inside mimicing a Buddhist temple: much is made of burgundy, deep woods, giant candles and Tibetan artefacts; music is strictly chanting monks, although a lama has probably never had a 'Himalayan Healing Stone Massage before. At least not legally. Other treatments include bathing in milk and smearing the body with honey and caviar.

In One Spa
Raffles Beijing Hotel, 33 Dong Chang'an Jie, Dongcheng; tel: 6523 0333; daily 7am–2am; subway: Wangfujing; map p.136 B4
The usual five-star spa treatment in dark wood and marble elegance. What sets In One Spa apart is the option to play your own music, nice if you are not into the tweeting birds or Enya-esque music favoured by spa CD libraries.

Westin Heavenly Spa
98 Financial Street, Xicheng; tel: 6629 7878; daily 9am–10pm; subway: Fuchengmen; map p.133 D1
One of Beijing's most luxurious spas. Treatments begin with a cup of white tea, followed by a dip in a whirlpool and end with two 'violet-infused dark chocolates'. For an empress twist, try the massage with jade rollers. Cixi swore by it.

performed simultaneously by two masseuses. Leave smelling like lemon grass.

Jihua Spa & Resort
Xiaotang Shan, Changping District; tel: 6178 2288; subway: taxi from Lishuiqiao
Jihua is like most of Beijing's hot springs; expect a little neon glam and sleaze mixed in with your hot tub experience. There are indoor and outdoor pools, massage and traditional Chinese medicinal techniques.

Oriental Taipan
Sunjoy Mansion, 6 Ritan Lu, Chaoyang; tel: 6502 5722; daily 11am–3am; subway: Jianguomen; map p.137 D4
This local chain gets good, but not rave, reviews and is a favourite of young expatriate women who come here for the facials. All therapies come with free snacks and juice. Don't expect miracles, but do expect good value.

Palm Springs Spa
Palm Springs International Apartments and Club, 8 Chaoyang Gongyuan Nanlu, Chaoyang; tel: 6539 8888 ext. 8080; daily 10am–midnight; subway: taxi from Gongti Beilu

This luxurious spa tries to recreate aspects of the Silk Road – you enter into a Bedouin tent. The Middle Eastern crossed with oriental intrigue continues through the VIP and spa suites. The services might not match the Silk Road prices, but if you want a novelty rub, Palm Springs has got it.

Hotel Spas
Anantara
The Commune by the Great Wall, The Great Wall (Shuiguan near Badaling), Yangqing County; tel: 8118 1888 ext. 5100
Anantara's claim to fame is that it is a stone's throw from the Great Wall. This luxury spa is hushed and relaxing, and staff are brisk, efficient and friendly. The usual list of high-end treatments are on offer: hot stone, Thai, Balinese, aromatherapy and Ayurvedic, as well as an Indian head massage and a special anti-ageing facial for men. Anantara is managed by Mandara Spa, which operates facilities in Thailand, the Middle East and the Maldives.

> It is always worthwhile trying to bargain, especially in the mid-range and cheaper establishments. Places such as Bodhi and Oriental Taipan also offer discounts if you come during the daytime on weekdays.

Parks and Gardens

Amid the boom of construction and rush of commerce, Beijing's green spaces are precious pockets of peace. From first light, residents head to parks to engage in a fascinating mixture of martial arts, breathing exercises, opera, ballroom dancing, badminton, hanging from trees and kite-flying. While many of the city's parks are modelled on the traditional Chinese garden rather than wild swathes of lawn to roll around and picnic on, they are great places to escape from the traffic and observe some local culture.

Beihai Park

1 Wenjin Jie (just northwest of the Forbidden City), Xicheng; tel: 6403 1102; daily 7am–8pm; entrance fee; subway: Tiananmen West; map p.134 A2

This beautiful park, once part of the former lakeside pleasure grounds of the imperial family, is now accessible to all. In the south of the park, with a separate entrance, is the **Round Town** (*Tuancheng*), one of three islands in the Northern Lake. The Mongols had this island landscaped, but only the trees remain from that time, all the architecture of the Yuan dynasty

Left: a few limitations to Beijing's park life.

having been destroyed. An exquisite 1.5m- (49ft-) wide nephrite container, in which Kublai Khan kept his wine, also survives; it stands next to the entrance of a pavilion with white marble pillars and a blue roof.

The second island, **Hortensia** (Jade Island or *Qionghuadao*) is even more impressive. A path from the main south gate leads to a bridge more than 600 years old. A twisting path leads up uneven steps to the 35m

Left: ethnic dancer at Beihai Park's Five Dragon Pavilion.

(114ft) **White Dagoba**, an onion-shaped shrine in the Tibetan style. On the northern side, a path leads through a labyrinth of stairs, corridors, pavilions and bizarre rock formations carved into grottoes intended to resemble the houses of Daoist saints, and goes steeply down to the lake shore, which is bordered by a long, semicircular covered walkway. From here, a ferry takes visitors to the **Five Dragon Pavilion** (*Wulongting*), on the northwest shore. These buildings from the Ming era are built in a zigzagging line over the water and connected by walkways. Emperors used to fish from this point. The path leads west from the waterfront to the **Tower of 10,000 Buddhas** (*Wanfolou*), built by the emperor Qianlong in the 18th century on the occasion of his mother's 80th birthday. The pure gold statuettes of Buddha that filled the niches inside the

96

Left: morning exercises at Beihai Park.

Earth – symmetrically opposite to Tiantan *(see p.99)* or Altar of the Heaven in the south – is a mellow space just north of the Lama Temple *(see p.121)*. There is plenty of open space, including patches of grass ideal for picnicking. Along with Longtan Park in the south, Ditan is famous for holding some of the biggest Spring Festival fairs.

SEE ALSO FESTIVALS, P.48

Fragrant Hills Botanical Gardens

Xiangshan, Haidian; tel: 6259 1283; entrance fee; daily 7am–5pm; subway: taxi from Xizhimen; map p.24

The big draw in these expansive gardens is the heated greenhouse decked out like a tropical jungle. There are also over 2,000 types of orchid, ancient bonsai trees and fruit blossoms in the spring. Look out for the **China Honey Bee Museum** on the west side of the gardens.

Fragrant Hills Park (Xiangshan)

Xiangshan, Haidian; tel: 6269 1155; entrance fee; daily 6am–6pm; subway: taxi from Xizhimen; map p.24

Not all parks have entrance tickets, but for those that do the cost is minimal, usually around RMB2, at most RMB5. If the park has ticketed tourist venues inside – such as Tiantan Park – it is worth buying an all-in-one ticket at the park gates.

---

tower were stolen – like so many other treasures – by European troops in 1900.

To the south stands what is probably the biggest pavilion in China, the **Miniature Western Heaven**

(Xiaoxitian), which was built in 1770 as a shrine to Guanyin, the goddess of mercy. A few steps to the east of the **Dragon Screen** *(Jiulongbi)* is the **Hall of the Celestial Kings** *(Tianwangdian)*, a Ming-dynasty workshop for the translation and woodblock-printing of Buddhist scriptures.

Ditan Park

2 Andingmen Dajie, Dongcheng; tel: 6421 4657; entrance fee; daily 6am–9pm; subway: Yonghegong; map p.134 C4

Ditan Park, or Altar of the

Below: breaktime in the sunshine.

Beihai Park's **Altar of the Silkworm** *(Xiancantan)* is one of the eight altars that played a large part in the ritual life of Ming and Qing emperors. Here the empress would come to perform a ceremony honouring the goddess of silkworms – the wife of the mythical Yellow Emperor, who supposedly discovered the secret of the silkworm – and to pray for a good harvest.

On a clear day this beautiful, sprawling park offers excellent views of the city you have left behind. In the Liao dynasty (907–1125), noble and wealthy merchant families built elegant villas on the cool slopes of these hills, to which they could flee when temperatures in the city soared. Later, the Ming emperors turned the area into an imperial game preserve. As recently as 300 years ago, the Qing emperor Kangxi is supposed to have killed a tiger here. Qianlong turned it into a landscaped park, a complex of 28 scenic zones, named the Park of Tranquillity and Pleasure. As with both of the Summer Palaces, however, it was badly damaged by foreign troops in 1860, and again in 1900. Few of the buildings have survived.

Bear in mind that on summer and autumn weekends the crowds are so large it can sometimes feel as if you are still in the city. The hills are particularly popular in

Right: traditional costume at Fragrant Hills Park.

Left: Fragrant Hills Park.

late autumn because of the blazing reds and yellows of the sycamore leaves.

Inside is a chairlift that will take you to the 550m (1,800ft) summit of the 'Fragrant Hill'. From here you can gaze over steep, thickly wooded slopes and deep ravines to **Biyunsi Temple** (in a side valley on the northeast side of the park). Further away is the **Jade Spring Hill**, with its ancient pagoda, with the **Summer Palace** and **Kunming Lake** beyond. In the far distance are the skyscrapers of Haidian District – on a clear day you can get a good impression of the immensity of Beijing. If you're feeling fit you can climb the hill on foot instead of taking the chairlift, but you will need good shoes and at least a couple of hours to spare. The steepest part of the hill bears the name *Guijianchou*, which means 'Even the devil is afraid of it!'

The southern part of the park beyond the **Xiang Shan Hotel** is excellent for picnics. Yet only a few visitors ever seem to find their way here.
SEE ALSO TEMPLES, CHURCHES AND MOSQUES, P.124–5

Park opening times usually follow sunlight hours. The times given here are for winter; in summer, parks tend to open an hour earlier and close an hour later. Note most parks will not allow you to bring your bicycle inside.

Jingshan (Coal Hill)

Wenjin Jie (directly behind the Forbidden City), Xicheng; tel: 6404 4071; entrance fee; daily 6.30am–8pm; subway: either of the Tiananmen stations; map p.134 A1
This is an artificial landform made from the dirt scooped out when Ming workmen were digging the Forbidden City's moat. Five pavilions, dating from the 16th century, crown the chain of hills and emphasise their zigzagging lines. Each pavilion once housed a bronze figure of Buddha, but four of these were plundered by European troops in 1900.

The locust tree where Chongzhen, the last Ming emperor, committed suicide in 1644, after the rebellious peasant armies walked into Beijing, is now a favourite photo spot for Chinese tourists. On a clear day you can see the silhouette of the Western Mountains from the **Pavilion of Everlasting Spring** *(Wanchungting)*, on the middle of the five peaks.

Longtan Park

8 Longtanhu Lu, Chongwen; tel: 6714 4336; entrance fee; daily 6am–9pm; subway: taxi from Tiantan Dongmen; map p.137 C1/D1
Longtan means dragon pool, and the park pays homage to its namesake with a menagerie of stone replicas of the mythical beast. Just east of the Temple of Heaven, there's a boating

Above: spring tulips bloom in Jingshan.

guomen; map p.137 D4

Ritan is the Altar of the Sun. The rebuilt altar still stands, and the rest of the park is a pleasant place for a stroll – with rocks, ponds and meandering paths, flower beds and several good tea-houses and restaurants. Look out for the **Stone Boat Café**, a bar and café on a platform over the lake.
SEE ALSO BARS, P.33

lake, open-air bird market and plenty of green. Famous for its Spring Festival Fair.

Purple Bamboo Park (Zizhuyuan Gongyuan)

45 Baishiqiao Lu, Haidian; tel: 6842 5851; daily 6am–8pm; subway: Xizhimen; map p.132 A3

Right next to the zoo, Purple Bamboo Park lives up to its name, with 10 different kinds of bamboo growing on its grounds. Boats can be hired to navigate this park's three interconnecting lakes and its bundle of canals. There is also a giant waterslide. The gardens are laid out in the classical Chinese style; look out for the **Purple Bamboo Pavilion** and the **Gallery for Watching the Moon**.

Ritan

6 Ritan Beilu, Chaoyang; tel: 8561 6301; daily 6am–9pm; subway: Jiang-

The quirky little **China Honey Bee Museum** is an interesting diversion within the Botanical Gardens. Anything remotely bee-related is on display, from bee fossils to ancient paintings depicting cavemen hunting for honey. There are also giant wild honeycombs. It's an apiarist's sweet dream.

Tiantan Park

Yongdingmennei Dajie (West Gate), Chongwen; tel: 6702 8866; daily 7am–9pm; entrance fee; subway: Tiantan Dongmen; map p.136 B2/C1

As well as the spectacular blue-tiled Ming-dynasty sacrificial halls, Tiantan is Beijing's biggest inner-city park. It is a favourite place for locals to practise t'ai chi. It is also very popular with men wielding traditional Chinese musical instruments or playing *weiqi* (Go) and Chinese chess. Come early in the morning before the tour groups arrive. Impromptu performances are usually held around the **Long Corridor**.

Zhongshan Park

1 Zhonghua Lu (west of Forbidden City), Xicheng; tel: 6605 5431; daily 6am–8pm; entrance fee; subway: Tiananmen West; map p.134 A1

Also called Sun Yat-sen Park, this is a fine example of the fusion of imperial architecture and garden design. Over 1,000 years ago this was the site of the Temple of the Wealth of the Land, but the ancient cypresses are all that remain from that time. From the main entrance to the park in the south, the path first goes through a white marble arch, inscribed with the line 'Defend peace', by poet Guo Moruo. Further north, in the centre of the park, is a great square area, where in 1421 the Ming Altar of Earth and Harvests stood. To the north of the altar is the **Zhongshan Hall** (formerly called the *Shejitian*, or Hall of Prayer), built of wood, a typical example of Beijing's classical architecture. Also inside the park is the Forbidden City Concert Hall, which puts on concerts by Western and Chinese orchestras.
SEE ALSO MUSIC, DANCE AND THEATRE, P.78

Below: Ritan's Stone Boat Café.

Restaurants

There is nothing the Chinese like more than eating out, and the range and number of restaurants in Beijing is testament to the capital's love of food. You can go high-class and blow RMB1,000 at a designer establishment or spend less than RMB20 on a hearty bowl of fresh noodles. Beijing is lucky to play host to myriad different cuisines from around the country, as well as a global spread of international restaurants from Ethiopian to Greek. Of course, no meat-eating visitor would miss the signature dish – the crispy, calorie-rich Peking duck.

Beijing Duck

Beijing Duck, Peking Duck, *kaoya*; whatever you like to call it: the city's namesake dish is made from slivers of crispy roast duck meat wrapped in a pocket-sized pancake, stuffed with spring onions (scallions) and cucumber and smeared with plum sauce. You can either opt for the bustling tourist hall, which has all the pomp and circumstance of roasting the birds for more than century, or the smaller establishment which, because it is not cooking for the masses, may dish up a tasty twist to the staple. The two famous 'historic' duck restaurants are **Quanjude**, established in 1864 – the Qianmen branch kept its fires burning even after the restaurant was closed as the street under-

went major redevelopment – and **Bianyifang**, which is Beijing's oldest duck restaurant and can trace its origins to 1416. **Beijing Da Dong** is a swanky chain that does duck to a tee but is not so hot on the rest of the menu, considering the bill. The Hyatt's **Made in China** *(see opposite)* does a modern twist to the roast meat and is sometimes voted the best place to eat roast duck in Beijing. **Li Qun**, now a staple on the tourist trail, does a – usually – great chaotic duck in a courtyard setting. While the service at Li Qun has had a few complaints, diners get to witness the roasting process.

Price codes are per person for an average three-course meal, with one beer or glass of wine.
$ under RMB50
$$ RMB50–100
$$$ RMB100–300
$$$$ over RMB300

Bianyifang
2 Chongwenmenwai Dajie, Chongwen, Along Chang'an Jie; tel: 6712 0505; daily 11am–2pm, 6–9pm; $$–$$$; subway: Chongwen; map p.136 C2

Li Qun Roast Duck Restaurant
11 Beixiangfeng, Zhengyi Lu, Qianmen, Southern Beijing; tel: 6705 5578; daily 10am–10pm; $$–$$$; subway: Qianmen; map p.136 B3

Quanjude
32 Qianmen Dajie, Southern Beijing; tel: 6701 1370; daily 11am–1.30pm, 4.30–8.30pm; $$–$$$; subway: Qianmen; map p.136 B3

Along Chang'an Jie

BEIJING
Yuebin
43 Cuihua Hutong (opposite the South Gate of the National Arts Museum), Dongcheng; tel: 8511 7853; daily 11am–2pm, 5–9pm; $–$$; subway: Dengshikou; map p.134 B1

Yuebin owes its fame to the fact that it is Beijing's first post-1949 private restaurant. The family gambled their life savings, roping in relatives and friends to run the kitchen back in 1980. Don't let its humble

Left: Quanjude.

2.30pm; $$$$; subway: Tiananmen East; map p.136 B4
Sitting next to the moat east of the Forbidden City, The Courtyard has nothing short of an imperial location. This fine-dining fusion restaurant is set in a renovated Qing-dynasty villa. Reviewers tend to rave at the décor, which is designer-chic meets ancient Asia, and the magical views of the palace. The food, however, may not always be worth the royal price tag.

The Lake District
BEIJING
Hutong Laozi
(no English sign)
9 Yingding Bridge Hutong (next door to Hutong Pizza), Xicheng; tel: 13269 251223 (no English spoken); daily 5–9pm; $; subway: Gulou; map p.134 A3
One of Beijing's best-kept secrets, eating here is literally like eating at a family home.

appearance – glass-topped tables, slightly off-colour walls – fool you. This place serves great family-style Beijing cooking and is cheap as chips as well as being a historical landmark. Their dumplings get a big thumbs up.

CHINESE
Made in China
Grand Hyatt Beijing, Oriental Plaza, 1 Dongchang'an Jie, Dongcheng; tel: 6510 9608; daily 7–10am, 11.30am–2.30pm, 5.30–10pm; $$$–$$$$; subway: Wangfujing; map p.136 B4
Eating here is like eating in a kitchen itself: the funky Japanese designers took the chefs and their equipment, put them behind glass and arranged the dining tables around them. It makes for an aroma-filled, wok-sizzling experience. For a classy restaurant like this, though, the tables are too close, and the kitchen action kills any hopes for an intimate meal. The food gets rave reviews – classic Chinese cuisine with a modern twist. Their Peking duck is consistently

voted the best in the city by the expatriate magazines.

FUSION
The Courtyard
95 Donghuamen Dajie, Dongcheng; tel: 6526 8883; daily 6–10pm, Sun also 11.30am–

Right: The Courtyard.

There's more to Mao kitsch than collecting copies of the *Little Red Book*. Beijing is currently going through a craze for restaurant revolutionary chic. All a proprietor has to do is dress his staff in Red Army uniforms, stick up some suitable Mao and Communist propaganda posters and perhaps throw in some revolutionary singing. **The East is Red** (266 Baijiaolou, Dong Wuhanwai, Chaoyang) is the crème de la crème of Communist dining, with rousing nightly floor shows and red flags for customers. **Guoqu Niandai Xiangcai Guan** (Second Ring Road opposite Gulou subway station; map p.134 A4) has gruff but helpful staff in olive-green army gear and serves creamy Hunan food. Finally, the upmarket and Western-run **Red Capital Club** (66 Dongsi 9 Tiao, Dongcheng; *right*) is a courtyard nook filled with 1950s Communist Party furniture, including a leather armchair that once supported the Great Helmsman's buttocks.

Hutong Laozi is run by an old Beijing couple: she serves, he cooks. The menu depends on what they can get from the market that day, and that excludes vegetables 'that are just too pricey this time of year'. The food, which is called 'home-cooking', is fresh, delicious and inexpensive – liquids are limited to soft drinks and beer. The couple love talking, are very friendly and light up the ambience of their simple front room.

FUSION
Ken de Rouge
22 Houhai Lake (west bank), Xicheng; tel: 6402 6665; daily 11am–10pm; $$$; subway: Jishuitan; map p.134 A3
Minimalist setting with grey floors, brick walls and flashes

of black and imperial red; it's true to say Ken de Rouge's big draw is its designer setting and breathtaking views of the lake rather than the food. The fusion fare has had mixed reviews, portions considered a little on the mean side and service a little slack for such steep prices. However, the wine list is long, and the menu should delight, with plenty of seafood, including lobster.

IMPERIAL
Fangshan Restaurant
Beihai Park (near East Gate), 1 Wenjin Jie, Dongcheng; tel: 6401 1889; daily 11am–1.30pm, 5–8pm; $$$$; subway: Tiananmen West; map p.134 A3
This novelty imperial dining hall has all the atmosphere – staff are straight out of the

Forbidden City and there is also an option for guests to graze in historical costume – but little of the royal standards in the kitchen. Imperial cuisine is made up of dishes whipped up for the emperor and his family and include venison and turtle and other offbeat meats. The food here is pricey – RMB500 for a place on their banquet – and is probably not worth it unless you accede you are paying for the experience. Book several days ahead.

Lijia Cai
11 Yangfang Hutong, Deshengmennei Dajie, Xicheng; tel: 6618 0107; $$$–$$$$; daily 6–10pm; subway: taxi from Jishuitan; map p.133 E3
The travel gourmets, led by *Conde Nast,* have long rated

this family-run imperial kitchen, indeed you might have trouble securing a reservation so popular is Lijia Cai. Set menus range from RMB200 to RMB2,000, and include everything from roast duck to sweet-and-sour pork to abalone.

SHANGHAI
Mei Mansion
24 Daxiangfeng Hutong (south bank of Houhai), Xicheng; tel: 6612 6847; daily 11am–2pm, 5–10pm; $$$-$$$$; subway: taxi from Zhangzizhonglu; map p.133 E3
Notoriously difficult to find, this charming courtyard restaurant, once the home of opera great Mei Lanfang *(see page 34)*, has a – rather steeply priced – set menu of delicate Shanghai cuisine. Try the petal-filled dumplings.

YUNNAN
No Name Restaurant
1 Da Jinsi Hutong (just west of Yinding Bridge), Houhai, Xicheng; tel: 6618 6061; daily 11am–midnight; $$–$$$; subway: Gulou; map p.134 A3
Quirky meets fine dining, No Name has a ground floor like a jewel-studded grotto and a

Price codes are per person for an average three-course meal, with one beer or glass of wine.
$ under RMB50
$$ RMB50–100
$$$ RMB100–300
$$$$ over RMB300

rooftop terrace that is strung with fairly lights at night and puts the romance back into Houhai. Portions may be a shade small, but the flavours are authentic Yunnan, lightly and delicately fragranced steamed lemon-grass fish is one of their signature dishes. Popular with trendy locals, No Name is a great mid-priced hideaway. A bottle of one of their South American wines can round off a good night.

ZHEJIANG
Kong Yi Ji
South Bank of Houhai, Xicheng; tel: 6618 4915; daily 11am–10pm; $$–$$$; subway: Jishuitan; map p.134 A3
Famous for its *zuixia* (drunken shrimp) – the creatures are drowned alive in boiling alcohol – Kong Yi Ji also dishes up moreish pumpkin cakes and lightly braised spring onions. Named after a character in a

Lu Xun novel *(see p.72)*, this restaurant is decked out like a nobleman's villa, with vases and rosewood furniture. The setting is complemented by some isolated (for Houhai) views of the lake.

Gulou
INDIAN
Mirch Masala
60–2 Nanluogu Xiang, Dongcheng; tel: 6406 4347; daily 11am–2.30pm, 5–10.30pm; $$; subway: Gulou, map p.134 B3
Many of the ingredients are flown in from Delhi, according to the owner, and you can taste the freshness in many of their dishes. This cosy, fairly cheap restaurant is probably the best on Nanluogu Xiang. Service is friendly, and their chicken vindaloo is the spiciest in Beijing. Good cheap draught beer; the only thing that is missing is an on-site bathroom.

ITALIAN
Passby Bar
108 Nanluogu Xiang, Dongcheng; tel: 8403 8004; 9.30am–2pm; $$; subway: taxi from Zhangzizhonglu; map p.134 B3

China's appetite for disposable chopsticks gobbles up more than 25 million trees each year. It's an environmental nightmare. Even the government is trying to do something about it. At the end of 2007, the Ministry of Commerce issued new guidelines urging restaurants to cut down on their use. When you visit Beijing, you can do your bit for the environment by bringing your own pair. Yashow Market *(see p.112)* sells wooden painted and collapsible metal chopsticks for less than RMB20.

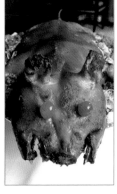

Left: cute, cuddly, edible.

25 Jiugulou Dajie, Xicheng; tel: 8403 6689; daily 11am–11pm; $$; subway: Gulou; map p.134 A3

You can gorge yourself at Phoenix Bamboo and not feel bad about it. Most of the dishes are composed of fresh vegetables, either lightly braised or served salad-raw, although they also have flavoursome fried chicken and fish dishes. Try the slightly chillied mint salad and the fresh buckwheat noodles with red cabbage. The service is keen but a bit haphazard, and there is no on-site bathroom, but that is par for the course around Gulou. The ambience is enhanced by some old

Passby was the first restaurant to set up shop on Nanluogu Xiang, and it is still madly popular today with travellers, locals and expatriates. The food is pleasant – pastas, pizza and some interesting salads – but it is the cosy courtyard feel that is attractive. In the evening indoors is a jumble of bookshelves and crooked tables.

SICHUAN
Ba Guo Bu Yi
89–3 Dianmen Dongdajie, Dongcheng; tel: 6400 8888; daily 10am–2pm, 5–9.30pm; $$; subway: Zhangzizhonglu; map p.134 B2

A chain from Chengdu that lures in diners with its fabulous *bian lian* (face-changing shows); an act from Sichuan Opera where the performer 'magically' flicks between brightly-coloured and often fearsome face masks. Shows, 15 minutes long, are only staged in the evening. This noisy, packed dining hall also serves great Sichuan food and will tone down the spices for the foreign palate. Their *dan dan mian* peanut-pork noodles and 'very spicy fish' are perennial favourites.

Private Kitchen No.44
44 Xiguan Hutong, Beixinqiao

Nan, Dongcheng; tel: 6400 1280; daily 11am–11pm; $$; subway: Zhangzizhonglu; map p.134 C2

This tumbledown hippy courtyard house with a little garden is a comfortable mishmash of ethnic paraphernalia and odd-shaped gourds. The menu is an extensive list of Guizhou favourites, the most popular dish being the sour spicy fish, which can be washed down with cups of *guihua* rice wine.

Source
14 Banchang Hutong, Dongcheng; tel: 6400 3736; daily 11am–2pm, 5.30–10.30pm $$; subway: Zhangzizhonglu; map p.134 B2

A gallery owner opened this elegant courtyard nook which is scooped out of a Qing dynasty nobleman's residence. In the summer, dinner can be taken in the courtyard under the pomegranate tree. The menu is a set meal of not-so-spicy Sichuanese food, which gets rave reviews from foreigners but is sometimes considered rather bland by locals who dig *mala*.

YUNNAN
Fenghuang Zhu
(Phoenix Bamboo – no English sign)

If you don't want meat, tell the waiter *wo bu chi rou*. But if you want to make really sure, head to one of Beijing's many vegetarian or vegan restaurants, which, in the best Buddhist tradition, magics tofu and wheat gluten into meat-and fish-like states. By far the best vegetarian restaurant in town for price and choice is **Still Thoughts** (18A Dafosi Dongjie; map p.134 B2) in an alley five minutes' walk north of the National Arts Museum. Tucked in a little hutong off Dongzhimen Beixiaojie, **Baihe** (23 Caohuang Hutong; map p.135 D3) is perhaps more elegant, set in a traditional Chinese courtyard, but the food is not as fabulous. **Xu Xiang Zhai** (26 Guozijian Jie; map p.134 C3), just east of the Confucius Temple, does a royal weekend lunchtime buffet spread and is popular with monks and nuns, while **Pure Lotus** (3/F Holiday Inn Lido) is designer vegetarian food in a beautiful Buddhist setting.

Chinese furniture and dim lighting. Dinner reservations recommended on weekends. Alternatively you can settle in at Jiangjinjiu Bar and eat from Phoenix Bamboo's kitchen there, as they are 100m (328ft) apart and have the same owner.

The Embassy District

BEIJING
Xiao Wang Fu
Ritan Gongyuan (inside the north gate of Ritan), Chaoyang; tel: 8561 7859; daily 11am–2.30pm, 5–10pm; $$$; subway: taxi from Chaoyangmen; map p.137 D4

Oft-cited as 'the best to take overseas visitors', this classy Chinese dining hall has fabulous views of the park on its rooftop terrace and a huge menu of local food. Particularly popular is their crisp-skinned roast duck.

BRAZILIAN
Alameda
Sanlitun Houjie, Nali Mall, off Sanlitun Beilu, Chaoyang; tel: 6417 8084; daily noon–3pm, 6–11pm; $$$; subway: Gongti Beilu; map p.135 E3
Always packed, this Brazilian slash European diner is

> If you want to sample the varied cuisine of China's regions, head to one of the restaurants associated with their representative offices. After all, top government officials eat here, they must be the best. For Yunnan, **Yunteng Shifu** (Donghuashibeili Dongqu, Chongwen; map p.137 C3) is a riot of green, teal and fairy lights, but has the heartiest mint salad and exquisite fish; authentic Sichuan fare can be had at **Chuan Ban** (5 Gongyuan Toutiao, Jianguomennei Dajie; map p.137 C4); while the heartiest Xinjiang is dished up the **Xinjiang Islam Restaurant** (7 Sanlihe Lu, Xicheng; map p.132 B2).

another favourite of expatriates who rave about its steaks and black-bean stew. Everything is set menu, with the lunchtime sets particularly good value. Recently changed ownership, so best to check local listing magazines to see if it is still on their top-ten lists. Its fierce popularity means it is not a place to come for an intimate night out: it is always crowded and everything is a bit of a squeeze.

Below: a gentrified hutong restaurant.

CHINESE
Purple Vine
28, Sanlitun, Chaoyang; tel: 6416 8855; daily 10am–2pm, 5–11pm; $$–$$$; subway: Gongti Beilu; map p.135 E2
Purple Vine is one-third restaurant, one-third tea-house and one-third furniture store. Dine off Qing-dynasty-style tables and chairs surrounded by antiques – elaborate screens, lacquered boxes and frayed costumes. The service is attentive, the food excellent and the atmosphere genteel.

FUSION
Muse
Chaoyang Ximen (West Gate of Chaoyang Park), Chaoyang; tel: 6586 3188; daily 10am–midnight; $$; subway: taxi from Gongti Beilu
This mod Parisian-Vietnamese canteen is one of Beijing's best restaurants for good, hearty, yet light fusion food. The funky black-and-red mirror-hung dining room is a little brashly lit, shattering any romance, but it's always lively, always busy and service is fast and friendly. Their speciality is a jumbo bowl of beef noodle soup called 'traffic lights', but the fish curry is heaven, the salads are tangy and there's a good choice of French wines.

JAPANESE
Yotsuba
Building 2, Xinyuanxili Zhongjie, Chaoyang; tel: 6467 1837; daily 5–9.30pm; $$$; subway: taxi from Dongzhimen

Price codes are per person for an average three-course meal, with one beer or glass of wine.
$ under RMB50
$$ RMB50–100
$$$ RMB100–300
$$$$ over RMB300

Left and below:
imperial presentation.

you are into that kind of thing, to watch the North Korean spooks, garbed in identical long black overcoats, as they enter and leave their private dining rooms. As one diner put it, 'I wish they had a souvenir stand.'

NORTHEAST CHINESE
Dongbei Ren
A1 Xinzhong Jie, Dongzhimenwai, Dongcheng; tel: 6415 2588; daily 11am–10pm; $–$$; subway: Dongzhimen; map p.135 D2

This Manchurian dumpling house is Beijing's most colourful restaurant – the stocky waitresses are dressed in traditional floral print, and the interior is a riot of reds to mimic the decorations for a wedding party. Dongbei Ren dishes up pretty good *jiaozi* (dumplings) to boot – try the wild vegetable vegetarian *jiaozi* and a feast of other Manchurian cuisine, including a monster sweet and

Yotsuba is generally considered to be Beijing's best Japanese restaurant. The tiny space – only two tatami rooms and a sushi bar – seats at most 30, and so reservations are required sometimes two or three days in advance. The fish and seafood are flown in fresh from Tokyo daily, and the chef pays great attention to detail and service – the fresh slices are dispatched a pair at a time exactly to match your eating pace. The fatty tuna and crab miso soup come highly recommended.

MALAYSIAN
Café Sambal
43 Doufuchi Hutong (off Jiugulou Dajie), Xicheng; tel: 6400 4875; daily 11am–midnight; $$–$$$; subway: Gulou; map p.134 A4

Dinner is eaten in individual rooms in a creaky little courtyard house. The main splendours here are the rich southeastern curries as well as the cosy candlelit atmosphere. Try the Kapitan chicken or the squid sambal. Not cheap, but Café Sambal's fare is flavoursome and filling.

NORTH KOREAN
Haitanghua Pyongyang
8 Xinyuanxili Zongjie, Chaoyang; tel: 6461 6295; daily 11am–2.30pm, 5–10.30pm; $$–$$$; subway: taxi from Dongzhimen

The attraction of this North Korean restaurant is not its food – it's merely a blander, more expensive version of South Korean fare – but in the surreal experience afforded by a meal here. All of the waitresses, half of them dressed in electric air-hostess blue and the other in shimmering *hangbok*, that formless sack the Koreans call national dress, are all from North Korea. They are charming, will pose for photos and guardedly tell you about life in Pyongyang. They also sing and play electric guitar at 7pm and 8pm. It is also enjoyable, if

YUNNAN
Middle 8
Building 8, Sanlitun Donglu, Sanlitun, Chaoyang; tel: 6413 0629; daily 11am–midnight; $$–$$$; subway: Gongti Beilu; map p.135 E2

Its funky white interior makes much of mirrors and red sofas. This very popular hip Yunnan restaurant is a little hectic, but the food is consistently good and well priced. The goat's cheese is delicious, but if you are hankering after something odd, try the deep-fried cactus.

sour fish that is deep-fried to a delicious crisp and comes with a happy folk song from the waiting staff.

SHANGHAI
Din Tai Fung
24 Xinyuanxili Zhongjie, Chaoyang; tel: 6462 4502; Sat–Sun 11am–10pm; $$$; subway: taxi from Dongzhimen

A Taiwanese chain that is considered to serve the city's best *xiaolongbao* – delicate pork-filled buns served in a basket. It is debatable whether they are Beijing's best, but they are certainly great, as are their tiny sweet red bean dumplings. Perennially popular, Din Tai Fung is a great place to take the family: it's spacious, clean and has a playpen for the children.

SICHUAN
South Beauty
4/F Oriental Kenzo Square, 21 Dongzhimenwai Zongjie, Dongcheng; tel: 8447 6171; daily 11am–10pm; $$–$$$; subway: Dongzhimen

Designer Sichuan food in chic settings at reasonable prices; this chain of spicy

Chinese eateries is famous for its flamboyant dishes; you may specify how fiery you want your food. There are private glass-walled dining rooms, and running water enhances the restaurant's *feng shui*. Interesting location to watch the urban socialites dine while you gobble down *kung po* prawns. (Also branches in Oriental Plaza, Pacific Century Place and China World.)

XINJIANG
Xinjiang Red Rose
7 Xingfu Yicun, off Gongti Beilu (opposite Worker's Stadium North Gate), Chaoyang; tel: 6415 5741; daily 11am–11pm; $$; subway Gongti Beilu; map p.135 E2

This rowdy Xinjiang eatery has been serving platters of mutton and other hearty dishes from the northwestern region of China for years. Its nightly belly-dancing shows are especially fun when drunken Westerners take to the stage. Its authenticity is proved by the number of Central Asian and Xinjiang customers who flock here every night.

Central Business District
EUROPEAN
Aria
China World Hotel, 1 Jianguomenwai Dajie, Chaoyang; tel: 6505 2266 ext. 36; daily 11.30am–midnight; $$$$; subway: Guomao; map p.137 E4

Another hotel-hosted establishment that scoops in the awards, Aria is an upmarket Mediterranean restaurant rated for its fabulous wine list, wicked cocktails and sumptuous food – the wagyu beef burger comes well recommended. Live jazz in the evenings and decadent desserts could keep you here until the early hours.

FUSION
People 8
18 Jianguomenwai Dajie (behind the Scitech Hotel), Chaoyang; tel: 6515 8585; daily 11.30am–2.30pm, 5.30–11.30pm; $$$–$$$$; subway: Guomao; map p.137 E4

People 8 is the eighth restaurant under the Taiwan-based Shintori brand. Customers are served trendy Taiwanese-Japanese dishes in a Zen-black setting. Overpriced?

framed portraits on the ceiling, votive candles, Hindu deities, you name it. Like many of Beijing's designer restaurants, the food, in this case Sichuan with some Western options, though good, never quite comes up to scratch. It's a great place, however, to sip a cocktail and spy on Beijing's celebrity set.

Western Beijing

BEIJING
Whampoa Club
23a Jinrongjie, Financial Street, Xicheng; tel: 8808 8828; $$$$; daily 11.30am–10pm; subway: Fuchengmen; map p.133 D1
This is one of the few classy designer establishments where the food gets reviews that match those won for its décor; world-acclaimed chef Jereme Leung's dressed-up Beijing food has some fierce fans. The menu morphs as Leung experiments: at one time minced pigeon and truffle-flavoured dumplings were on the menu. Just as impressive is the interior to this lush courtyard restaurant. The walls are painted black, the space is hung with a crazy curtain of bird-cages, while fish swim overhead in a pond astride the glass ceiling.

Perhaps, although the sushi has some fans. But apart from the design, it's People 8's puzzles that give it an edge. Their big task is in hiding the toilets. Good luck in finding them.

JAPANESE
Hatsune
Heqiao Building, Building C, A8 Guanghua Donglu, Chaoyang; tel: 6581 3939; daily 11.30am–2pm, 5.30–10pm; $$$–$$$$; subway: Guanghua Lu; map p.137 D4
Like a slicky oiled machine, Hatsune wheels in its customers, wows with its variety of inventive rolls, whips up

orders in a trice and wheels them out again. This place is so popular it is hard not to be breathless when dining here. The prices are steep, but the food is great. Hatsune seems to be every expatriate's favourite Japanese in town, except for the Japanese, who prefer Yotsuba over this American-style sushi joint. Reservations are essential.

SICHUAN
LAN
4/F LG Twin Towers, 12B Jianguomenwai Dajie, Chaoyang; tel: 5109 6012; www.lanbeijing.com; daily 11am–late; $$$$; subway: Jianguomen; map p.137 E4
This Philip Starck-designed Cinderella palace must have been fun to put together. Taking up an entire floor of the LG tower, the pad is literally crammed with 'stuff' – bronze eagles in flight,

ITALIAN
Cepe
The Ritz-Carlton Beijing, 1 Jin Cheng Fang Street East, Financial Street, Xicheng; tel: 6601 6666; daily 11.30am–2.30pm, 6–10.30pm; $$$$; subway: Fuchengmen; map p.139 D4
So many awards have been showered on this fancy Northern Italian restaurant – one of *Forbes*'s Top Power Dining Spots of 2007 and

Price codes are per person for an average three-course meal, with one beer or glass of wine.
$ under RMB50
$$ RMB50–100
$$$ RMB100–300
$$$$ over RMB300

A growing number of successful (and not-so-successful) artists are trying their hand at the restaurant business. The big daddy of the paint world, **Ai WeiWei**, opened his minimalist **Qu Nar** (16 Dongsanhuan Beilu; map p.135 E4) as a place to hang out with his bohemian friends back in 2005. Prices are not astronomical, and by all accounts its Zhejiang fare is pretty good. The Cultural Revolution-chic Sichuan café **Tianxaiyan** (Dashanzi), opened by photographer **Cang Xin**, also gets good reviews for its spicy meats and tofu. **Fang Lijun's** super-hip **South Silk Road** (Soho New Town, Jianguo Lu) serves very good Yunnan food, and photographer **Chen Nong** has just reopened his scruffy **Here Café** (upper Yu'er Hutong just off Nanuogu Xiang; map p.134 B2), where he displays his trademark hand-coloured photography. Finally, **Three Guizhou Men** (inside Worker's Stadium, West Gate; map p.135 D2) was opened by three Guizhou artists who found it more lucrative to make food than paintings. *See also Museums and Galleries, p.77.*

runner-up in local magazine *That's Beijing's* Best Italian, Best Restaurant, Best Décor and Best Service in the same year – that Cepe must be doing something right. Diners rave about the porcini mushrooms grown in their in-house humidor, the rich wine list and the cute Italian cooks.

The North

EUROPEAN
The Orchard
Hegezhuang Village, Cuigezhuang Township, Shunyi; tel: 6433 6270, 1391 121 1965; Tue–Sun noon–2.30pm, 6–9pm; $$$; subway: taxi from airport
This little expatriate heaven is probably best sampled on a weekday to avoid the exuberant children of other diners. Fresh organic produce, rich European cooking and a good, strong wine list served either in the elegant dining rooms or the tree-filled garden. Arrange return transport in advance, as The Orchard is quite isolated.

Right: the friendly staff at the Red Capital Club, *see p.102.*

YUNNAN
Golden Peacock Dai Ethnic Flavour
16 Minzu Daxue Beilu, Weigongcun, Haidian; tel: 6893 2030; daily 11am–10pm; $$; subway: taxi from Xizhimen
Dai ethnic food, which tastes like a cross between Thai and Chinese and something else, is done to chunky perfection here. It's not for the calorie-shy – big pineapples hollowed out and filled with sticky purple rice, deep-fried bananas and fried potato balls are heavy going yet scrumptious. Golden Peacock is hugely popular with locals and savvy expats but it is still very down-to-earth. You might have to wait for a table, but it is definitely worth the trouble.

Shopping

A s the capital, Beijing is the shopping
epicentre of this enormous country.
Designer labels, local talent, and the sweep
of ethnic crafts from Tibet to Mongolia can
be found in markets, stalls and high-end shops
across the city. For visitors, silk, jade, *cloisonné*,
lacquerware, jewellery, carpets, watercolour
paintings and clothing all make popular gifts
or souvenirs to take home. Half the fun of
shopping in Beijing is in trawling through the
markets and bargaining for what you want. The
city is also famous for its underground trade in
pirated products: CDs, DVDs and luxury goods.

Shopping Areas

Most of the top hotels are
paired with elegant shopping
arcades. But the most interesting and inexpensive way
to spend your money is to
wander around one of the
main shopping areas, such
as **Wangfujing**, **Xidan** or
Qianmen. Here you will find
the more typical boisterous
shopping atmosphere. Many
of the people you see browsing are not Beijing residents
but visitors from other regions
on holiday or business.

You might be forgiven if
some of the malls remind
you of home; scores of overseas brands have set up
shop in Beijing. And more
are coming. Marks and
Spencer, Top Shop, Acces-
sorize, Banana Republic,
Gap and Urban Outfitters are
all rumoured to be Beijing-
bound in the next year or so.

GULOU

Gulou's old hutong are like
honey to owners of bou-
tiques and funky gift shops.
Local and overseas designers inject a little peasant or
Communist kitsch into their

creations. **Yandai Xiejie**, the
lane running east from
Houhai Lake's Yingding
Bridge, has Mao memora-
bilia, Tibetan fabrics and jewellery, silks, souvenirs and
hippy fashions. Musical
instruments – modern and
ancient – and urban street-
wear dominate **Gulou
Dongdajie**, while quirky local
designers have elbowed their
way into **Nanluogu Xiang**.
Three of the best to look out
for here are **Grifted** at No. 32
(www.grifted.com.cn), which
peddles cheeky Mao dolls
and stationery, **Plastered** at
No. 61 (www.plasteredtshirts.com),

Left: once this was the only
place for foreigners could shop
for luxury goods.

a Brit-owned local legend
that sells iconic t-shirts – look
out for their 'expat wanker'
range – and the **Cloth Art**,
No. 10. Their simple duo-
colour designs on fabric take
their inspiration from ethnic
religious motifs.

QIANMEN

Qianmen Dajie runs south
from Qianmen Gate at the
southern end of Tiananmen
Square. This was part of Beijing's busiest commercial
quarter during the Qing
dynasty. The whole area is
undergoing a US$40 million
renovation in the style of
1920s Beijing, and will open
complete with trams, opera
houses and some modern
twists, including China's first
Apple store and a Starbucks,
in mid-2008.

Corkscrewing southwest,
Dazhalan (Large Wicker
Gate) dates from the Ming
dynasty and remains one of
the liveliest shopping streets
in Beijing. Among the high-

Left: Oriental Plaza.

and brilliant wood-block prints. You can find expensive, as well as many cheap, souvenirs and gifts, including nice stone rubbings. This is also a good place to buy artist's materials. But genuine antiques have become scarcer and are generally limited to the more expensive shops.

SANLITUN
Sanlitun is not only good for boozing, it also has a good crop of shops. The **3.3 Shopping Mall** has trendy local boutiques and household designs, including An De Li Si on the fourth floor, which sells handmade shoes. **Nali Mall** across the road has funky silverware and jewellery stores, a good 'off the back of a lorry' shoe shop, **Long.com**, and more girly boutiques.

WANGFUJING
Beijing's premier shopping street is a pedestrian-only haven that has two of China's biggest shopping centres filled with luxury fashion brands, the **Sun Dongan**

Shops generally open from 9 or 10am–8pm or later every day. In department stores, chain stores and larger shops, prices are usually fixed, but bargaining is definitely expected elsewhere. Note that luxury goods and electronics are not a great bargain in Beijing; import duties and value added taxes add as much as 35 percent to the bill.

lights of the narrow lane is **Ruifuxiang**, an old silk shop with a marble gate and a traditional wooden interior. On the same street is the capital's best-known traditional pharmacist, **Tongrentan Pharmacy**, which dates from the mid-17th century. Dazhalan and the streets around it have a long history as an entertainment centre. Five of the biggest Beijing Opera houses used to be here, and you can still buy opera clothes, masks and props at the **Beijing Opera Costume Shop**. Two old shoe shops, **Neiliansheng**

and **Buyingzhai**, make traditional handmade cotton shoes. Mao ordered his cotton shoes from Dazhalan.

If you take a right turn off Dazhalan, you can continue west to **Liulichang**, famous for its antiques and art-and-craft items. You can buy original paintings and wood-block print reproductions, materials for traditional Chinese painting, and old (and new) books. Be prepared to bargain. The street runs east–west either side of Nanxinhua Jie. The most famous shop, **Rongbaozhai**, is on the western stretch and is known for its paintings, calligraphy

Suits You Sir
Beijing has some fine tailors and also some cheap-as-chips mediocre seamsters. Best to bring a copy of the design you want them to make or a picture from a magazine, as their own designs might be a bit 'yesterday'. It's also a good idea to buy your fabric from a separate stall, that way you'll at least limit your chances of getting overcharged. There are some classy tailors in the **Kerry Centre** *(see p.18)* and **China World Trade Centre Shopping Mall** *(see p.113)*. Cheaper options are in the **Friendship Store** *(see p.16)* and the third floor of **Yashow Market** *(see p.112)*.

Right: wood-block prints.

Plaza and the **Oriental Plaza** *(see opposite)*, at either end. Along the busy street are a few ancient shops, including **China Star Silk Store** (No. 133), **Beijing Medical Department Store** (No. 153), the refurbished **Beijing Department Store** (No. 255) and the **Wuyutai Teahouse** (No. 186).

XIDAN

Xidan is an old commercial quarter about a mile west of Tiananmen Square. It is very popular with Beijing's youth and is basically a forest of massive shopping malls packed with cheap fashions, urban clothing and 'lifestyle' designs, as well as upmarket shopping centres selling fashion togs and perfume. Two buildings of note are the **Xidan Science and Technology Mall**, which sells genuine mobile phones, and the **Beijing Books Building**, which has English-language

---

Best place to buy…
Antiques: Panjiayuan *(see right)*
Designer clothing: Shin Kong Place *(see right)*
Pearls: Hongqiao *(see right)*
Fake brands: Silk Street *(see right)*
Buddhist merchandise: Shops opposite Lama Temple *(see p.121)*
Cotton shoes: Dazhalan *(see p.110–11)*
Electronics: Zhongguancun *(see p.112)*
Souvenirs: Yashow *(see p.112)*
Quirky souvenirs: Nanluogu Xiang *(see p.110)*
Books: Foreign Languages Bookstore *(see p.73)*
Silk: Ruifuxiang on Dazhalan *(see p.111)*
Tea: Wuyutai Teahouse *(see above)*
Carpets and rugs: Beijing Curio City *(see right)*

Right: Yashow Market.

titles in its basement. Come here on a weekday; weekends are heaving.
SEE ALSO LITERATURE, P.73

ZHONGGUANCUN

Zhongguancun is Beijing's 'Silicon Valley' and is dedicated to selling all kinds of gadgets, from laptop computers to electronic dictionaries. Note that Beijing is neither particularly cheap for electronics nor safe considering the number of fakes. Locally made brands, while super-cheap are definitely not made to last.

Markets

Hongqiao

Tiantan Donglu, Xuanwu; daily; subway: Tiantan Dongmen; map p.136 C2

Located across the road from the Temple of Heaven (eastern side), Hongqiao sells a bewildering variety of food, shoddily made electronics, clothes and antiques, but what people come here for are its pearls and stones clustered on the third floor. You will find strings of pearls by the hundreds, at a fraction of their cost in the West. Bargain hard.

Panjiayuan

Dongsanhuan Nanlu, Chaoyang; daily, but busiest at weekends; subway: taxi from Guo Mao; map p.137 E1

Close to the southeast corner of the Third Ring Road, Panjiayuan is one of the best places to buy genuine and reproduction antiques, as well as crafts, jewellery, furniture, old books and souvenirs of all kinds. Largely a weekend affair, Panjiayuan is already bustling by 6am, which is why some locals call it the 'Ghost Market'. However, the market is now so big and so established – with 3,000 fixed stalls – that any lingering ghosts

have no doubt left for quieter haunts. Bargaining is expected. It starts to close by mid-afternoon. Just to the south is **Beijing Curio City**, a four-storey complex with a huge range of antiques. Prices are a little higher than at Panjiayuan.

Silk Street Market

Jianguomenwai Dajie, Chaoyang; daily; subway: Yonganli; map p.137 E4

The Silk Street Market, once a narrow alley on Xiushui Jie next to Yonganli subway station, is now housed in a four-storey building next to its original location. It is famous for its knock-off labels: everything from Northern Face to Prada, although it has comically just released its own 'silkstreet' brand. Anyone who copies that, it warns, will be severely punished, blithely ignorant of the irony. Its upper floors are stacked with silks, tailors, souvenirs and jewellery.

Yashow

Gongren Tiyuchang Beilu, Chaoyang; subway: Gongti Beilu;

Right: Hongqiao pearls, spiritual statuettes and a modern setting.

Depending on how you look at it, bijou-purveyor **Shard Box** (1 Ritan Beilu, map p.135 D1) is either using a distasteful gimmick or is creating beauty out of tragedy. Each intricately crafted piece, from thumb-sized boxes to bold pendants, supposedly features shards of porcelain broken during the Cultural Revolution.

daily; map p.135 E2

Yashow is a five-storey market near Sanlitun. It is full of small stalls that sell clothing, souvenirs, toys, cosmetics, silk objects, books and just about everything else a tourist in Beijing might want to buy. The fifth floor is an eatery with inexpensive snacks. Most of the name-brand clothes are undoubtedly fakes, but dedicated shoppers will find much to look at here. As always, strong bargaining is both expected and required.

Shopping Malls

There are now more luxurious shopping malls in Beijing than you can shake a credit card at. And there are dozens more waiting to open. Park Life in the Central Business District's Yintai Centre, and scheduled to open in March 2008, will have the now familiar luxurious line-up of Cartier, Dolce & Gabbana, Donna Karan and Jean-Paul Gaultier.

China World Trade Centre Shopping Mall
1 Jianguomenwai Dajie, Chaoyang; subway: Guo Mao; map p.137 E4

China World, another long-stayer, has the full wardrobe of luxury clothing brands, the **China World Hotel** and its associated fine restaurants.

SEE ALSO HOTELS, P.65

Golden Resources Shopping Mall (Jinyuan Shangcheng)
69 Banjinglu, Haidian; subway: taxi from Xizhimen

This enormous mall is reputedly one of the largest in the world, with literally hundreds of escalators; word has it that if a shopper were to spend just 10 minutes in each of the Mall's shops, it would still take 90 hours to get through it.

Lufthansa Centre
52 Liangmaqiao Lu, Chaoyang; subway: Nongzhanguan

This high-end shopping centre was among the first Western-style malls to open its doors in the capital.

Oriental Plaza
1 Dongchang'an Dajie, Chaoyang; subway: Wangfujing; map p.136 B4

The pink-glassed Oriental Plaza has high-street clothing stores such as Levi's and Jack Jones, as well as exclusive retailers like Tiffany & Co. and chic-Chinoiserie clothing by Shanghai Tang.

The Place
9A Guanghua Lu, Chaoyang; subway: Yong An Li; map p.137 D4

The Place is noteworthy for its trippy digital canopy. Inside are mid-range brands such as Spain's Zara and Britain's French Connection, and a basement of foodcourts.

Season's Place
2 Jinchengfangjie, Financial Street, Xicheng; subway: Fuxingmen; map p.139 D4

This newcomer plays host to Hong Kong's Hyatt of department stores, Lane Crawford, which has a concierge on every floor.

Shin Kong Place
87 Jianguo Lu, Chaoyang; subway: Dawanglu; map p.

This is another slice of transplanted Hong Kong in Dawang Lu, just east of Guomao. Shin Kong's six floors are packed with 100 luxury brands, including Gucci's massive flagship store.

Sports

The 2008 Summer Olympics has thrown China's spotlight on sport, but with pollution often at the lung-tingling level, the average Beijing resident is usually content with a morning spell of t'ai chi or an indoor bout of ping pong. However, the capital does have a growing sporty side. As the city becomes more internationalised, western sports such as Aussie rules football and Brazilian Jiujitsu have appeared alongside the home-grown kung fu and kite-flying. In the winter, there is ice skating, skiing and snowboarding, and the Beijing Marathon is held each October.

Football

Football (soccer) has overtaken basketball as the most popular spectator sport in China. Naturally, the capital has one of the top professional football teams, Beijing Guo'an. Like many Chinese teams, Guo'an regularly attracts crowds of more than 50,000. They have also bought several foreign players, though the overall level of skill remains far behind that of leading European and South American teams. It is nonetheless worth watching a game to sample the unique atmosphere. Unfortunately – or perhaps fortunately – most visitors will not understand the crude chants. Tickets for Guo'an football matches can be bought from the ticket office on the north side of the Workers' Stadium (tel: 6592 1173).

Hiking and Cycling

The Beijing area offers plenty of opportunities for hiking and cycling. The Ming Tombs, Eastern Qing Tombs and Chengde are all set in picturesque hiking country, as are the Huairou and Miyun dis-

The Beijing International Marathon

Every October thousands of runners gather in the early hours of the morning at Tiananmen Square to take part in the annual Beijing marathon.

tricts north of the city. Beijing has several active hiking clubs which arrange weekend hikes. Try **Beijing Hikers** or the less hectic **Beijing Amblers**. Both clubs run full-day hikes to sites of natural and historical beauty. Camping equipment can be rented from the **Sanfo Outdoor Club**.

Cycling is also a great way to see parts of Beijing. **Cycle China** rents bikes and arranges trips out to the Great Wall. If you are looking for more hard-core pedalling, try the **Mountain Bikers of Beijing**, who get together to rough it on dirt tracks every Saturday. Helmets are compulsory.

SEE ALSO WALKS AND VIEWS, P.128–9

Beijing Amblers
Tel: 6432 9341; www.chinese cultureclub.org

Beijing Hikers
Tel: 13810 165056; www.beijing hikers.com
Cycle China
Tel: 6402 5653;
www.cyclechina.com
Mountain Bikers of Beijing
http://themob.404.com.au
Sanfo Outdoor Club
1/F Jinzhiqiao Mansion, Jianguomenwai Dajie; tel: 6507 9298; www.sanfo.com; subway: Guo Mao; map p.137 E4

Horseback Riding

While Chinese Mongolians have largely abandoned their nomadic life on horseback, wealthy expats and locals have started patronising **equestrian** clubs in suburban Beijing. **Cycle China** (see Hiking and Cycling above) also offers horseback-riding day trips. If you would rather spend a day at the races, fingers crossed the capital may reopen its **Beijing Jockey Club** tracks if a horse-racing 'trial' in Wuhan in 2008 goes according to plan. Beijing closed down the Tongzhou tracks in the east of the city in 2005 because of

Left: kites have been made in China for at least 2,500 years.

cation device, in fighting competitions and just as a way to relax. Every spring, Beijing hosts its own **Kite Festival** in Mentougou district.

Kung Fu

If you like what you see at the **Legend of Kung Fu** show, you can get in a few pointers by taking classes at one of the city's many kung fu schools. One of the largest and best established is the **Beijing Milun School of Traditional Kung Fu**, which, offers five different disciplines, including the monk-busting Shaolin and Shanda (a type of Chinese kick-boxing) at their Wangfujing courtyard. If you fancy something a little more relaxing, such as the slow-motion t'ai chi, which incorporates mediation techniques, the school holds classes in Ritan.

SEE ALSO MUSIC, DANCE AND THEATRE, P.81

Beijing Milun School of Traditional Kung Fu
3 Xitangzi Hutong (off Wangfujing), Chaoyang; Tel: 139 1072 4987; www.kungfuinchina.com; subway: Dengshikou; map p.134 B1

rampant illegal gambling. The country is now considering legalising betting on the horses.

Equuleus International Riding Club
Sunhe Town; tel: 6432 4694; www.equriding.com

Ice-Skating and Skiing

Come winter Beijing has lots of options for snowboarding, skiing and skating. Once it gets cold enough the skates (and sledge-equipped chairs and bikes) come out on Houhai, Qianhai and Beihai. Nanshan Ski Village and Shijinglong are the most popular ski and toboggan resorts. You can make your own way there or look in the expatriate magazines; they often run weekends away at Nanshan, including a stay at a log cabin. For those serious about their snow sports, a word of warning: the equipment looks more hand-me-down than state-of-the-art.

Right: skating at the China World Trade Centre, see p.113.

Nanshan Ski Resort
Shengshuitou Village; tel: 8909 1909; www.nanshanski.com
Shijinglong Ski Resort
Zhongyangfang Village; tel: 6919 1617; www.sjlski.com

Kite-Flying

Kite-flying is a popular pastime for all ages, especially in parks and in Tiananmen Square. Traditionally kites are made from silk or paper, but nowadays plastic is also used. Kites have been used in times of war as a communi-

China has a healthy population of 'polar bears' – that is, people with a penchant for swimming in freezing water. They plunge into holes in the ice, swearing by its medicinal and character-enhancing properties, despite the polluted state of the water. The best place in Beijing to spot a 'polar bear' is at Houhai. These usually retirement-aged men strip down to trunks, don goggles and caps, and perform enthusiastic breaststroke, churning up the frigid water while onlookers dressed in thick coats, scarves and hats, gasp in horror.

115

Teahouses

The Chinese have been drinking tea for more than 4,000 years. Growing it, selecting it, preparing it, and drinking it has been honed to a fine art. Tea is a social drink, a medicinal drink and even a religious drink – Buddhist monks mix their tea with meditation. The refined tea ceremony became popular in the Tang dynasty, but it wasn't until the final imperial chapter, the Qing dynasty, that people started adding performance art – opera and acrobatics – to their drinking time, thus spawning the slapstick teahouse culture which still exists today.

Down to a Tea

At its simplest there are three different kinds of tea – green, oolong and black. Infused teas are green or black teas that have been 'perfumed' with fruit or flower oils such as jasmine. All tea comes from the same plant, *Camilla sinensis*, native to China; how the leaves are then processed determines what kind of tea it is. Green teas (the most popular brew in China) are non-fermented; oolong is semi-fermented; while black tea (such as English Breakfast) is fully fermented. Generally the more fermented a tea is, the more caffeine it contains. Herbal tea is made from the leaves of flowers and herbs and not *Camilla*, and so strictly speaking it is not a real tea, although similar processes are used to extract the flavour.

Some famous Chinese teas to look out for are: *Longjing* (Dragon Well), a green variety grown in the Hangzhou Mountains; *Tie Guanyin* (Iron Goddess of Mercy), an oolong brew that

goes well with biscuits; and *Pu'er*, usually carefully aged bricks of strong black tea. *Molihua* is a green tea scented with jasmine flowers, while *juhua* (chrysanthemum tea) is a herbal drink that is said to calm the nerves.

Chinese take their tea very seriously, similar to the attention given to wines in the West. It is worthwhile just to visit one of Beijing's famous tea shops with its giant jars of leaves and to take in the rich aroma. Some of the fancier shops allow you to taste before you buy. The most famous teashop is

Left: Chinese take their tea very seriously, similar to the attention given to wines in the West.

Wuyutai, which has branches all over the city. Other places to pick up a brew are **Maliandao** or Tea Street, which has eight wholesale tea markets and more than 600 tea shops, just south of the West Railway Station, and Taiwanese chain **Tian Fu Jituan**, or Dazhalan tourist street just south of Qianmen.

The Tea Ceremony

Chinese have been perfecting the art of drinking tea since the Tang dynasty, when scholar Lu Yu wrote his famous *Classic of Tea (Chajing)*. Teahouses foster an elegant atmosphere: gentle lighting, traditional music and servers, usually female, in costume, to prepare and pour the brew. Tea ware is usually made from unglazed clay and sits on a slatted bamboo tray to drain off the excess water. Each tiny cup holds about three mouthfuls of tea. At the beginning of the ceremony

Left: unglazed pots are used in the traditional tea ceremony.

Wufu, which means 'five happinesses' is a popular chain of teahouse open until midnight. Tea is poured from purple sand teapots, a variety which reportedly helps retain the flavour of a brew.

Teahouse Theatre

Theatre teahouses are very different to the establishments which perform tea ceremonies. They are raucous, slapstick affairs, where customers sit around noisy tables, grazing on snacks such as rice cakes and dough twists, and tea is drunk in porcelain bowls or glasses and filled by waiters carrying brass teapots with remarkably long spouts. Performances run the gamut from Beijing Opera to acrobatics, from magic tricks to men pretending to be birds.

Lao She Teahouse

Building 3, Qianmen Xidajie, Xuanwu; tel: 6303 6830; subway: Qianmen; map p.136 A3
A great place to go if you want to catch a medley of different folk art in one fell swoop. This famous teahouse is named after novelist Lao She, who was persecuted to death during the Cultural Revolution. Doors close at 10pm.

Tibetans are also big tea-drinkers. It helps keep them warm on the plateau and aids digestion. Because of their nomadic roots, they favour easily portably brick tea, a black leaf that is compressed into a block. To this they add hot water, yak butter and salt. Beijing has a growing number of Tibetan restaurants and cafés where you can sample the unique taste of yak butter tea.

the cups are first doused with hot tea, which is then poured over the teapot to ensure the outside is at the same temperature as the inside. Hot water is again poured into the pot, allowed to sit for about 30 seconds, poured into cups and then drunk. With each infusion, 30 seconds to the brewing time is added.

Confucian Tea House

28 Guozijian Jie, Dongcheng; tel: 8404 8539; subway: Yonghegong; map p.134 C3
One of the friendliest teahouses in town, opposite the Confucius Temple. Staff give free lessons in English in the art of tea, and there is wireless Internet with every cup.

Family Fu's Teahouse

Houhai Lake (on the upper western bank), Dongcheng; tel: 6616 0725; subway: Jishuitan; map p.133 E3
Rather more regal than the other teahouses, Fu's has beautiful period furniture and glorious views of Houhai Lake.

Wufu Tea Ceremony House

20 Fuchengmenwai Dajie, Xicheng; tel: 6803 6467; subway: Fuchengmen; map p.132 C1

Beware the Chinese Tea Scam!

This scam is now well publicised, but it appears hapless tourists are still being taken in. The scammers, often posing as English students, lurk around Tiananmen or Wangfujing, inviting tourists to a teahouse. After a few cups, the scammers excuse themselves and the tourist is left with an inflated bill.

Right: traditional tea server.

117

Temples, Churches and Mosques

Although Daoism is the only major religion to have originated in China, the nation has absorbed all the world's main faiths over the centuries and is now home to millions of Buddhists, Muslims and Christians. They have all left their stamp on the capital, with dozens of temples, churches and mosques scattered around the city. Despite government control over religion, activities in places of worship go on pretty much as normal. Churches hold Sunday services, and monks continue to lodge at temples.

Along Chang'an Jie

St Joseph's (East Cathedral or Dongtang)
74 Wangfujing Dajie, Dongcheng; tel: 6524 0634; subway: Wangfujing; map p.134 B1
This Gothic-style cathedral was originally constructed back in 1655. It was razed to the ground in 1900 and had to be rebuilt. Today it holds Sunday services in English and Chinese. The front courtyard is a favourite practising ground of Beijing's less talented teen skateboarders.

The veneration of ancestors is one of the oldest practices in the Chinese spiritual tradition, hingeing on the belief that the well-being of the dead is dependent on the offerings and veneration of the living. The dead, in turn, are thought to be able to influence the fate of the living. The imperial ancestors received extraordinary honours and respect, of course, as they were believed to be responsible for the well-being of the whole country.

St Michael's
13A Dongjiaomin Xiang, Dongcheng; tel: 8511 5405; subway: Qianmen; map p.136 B3
Buried deep in the Legation Quarter, this Catholic Church, which was built by the French Vincentian Fathers in 1902, was nearly destroyed during the Cultural Revolution. It was renovated in 1989.

Southern Beijing
The Temple of Heaven
Yongdingmennei Dajie (West Gate), Chongwen; tel: 6702 8866; daily 8am–5.30pm (park 7am–9pm); entrance fee; subway: Tiantan Dongmen; map p.136 B1
Built in 1420, the Temple of Heaven served as a place of ritual for Ming and Qing emperors. Every year at the time of the winter solstice the emperor would come here in a magnificent procession lasting several days, in order to honour his ancestors and to pray for a good harvest in the season to come. As the Son of Heaven, the emperor administered heavenly authority on earth. Natural catastrophes, bad farming prac-

Above: St Joseph's Cathedral.

tices, failing harvests and increasing corruption were all signs that the emperor had lost the favour of Heaven and of his ancestors. In such circumstances, it was considered a legitimate act to overthrow him. Exact attention to the practice of the sacrificial rites in the Temple of Heaven was therefore given the appropriate importance by the ever-wary emperor.

The emperor changed his robes in the **Hall of Heaven** (Huangqiongyu). Built in 1530 and restored in 1730, this hall has a round, pointed roof with

Left: down-to-earth rituals at the Temple of Heaven.

level surrounded by a balustrade. The pointed roof, with its three levels, its 50,000 blue-glazed tiles – blue symbolises Heaven – and its golden point, was constructed without using a single nail and has no spars or beams. It is supported by 28 wooden pillars; the central four, the Dragon Fountain Pillars, are almost 20m (60ft) tall and represent the four seasons. The first ring of pillars surrounding them represents the 12 months; the outer ring, also of 12 pillars, the 12 divisions of the day. In the centre of the floor is a marble plaque with veining showing a dragon and a phoenix (symbolising the emperor and the empress).

To the east are more imperial buildings and the **Long Corridor**, a favoured spot for elderly musicians.

The Lake District

Guang Hua Si (Guanghua Temple)
31 Ya'er Hutong, Xicheng; tel: 6403 5032; daily 8am–4pm; subway: Gulou; map p.134 A3
Tourists may only visit some parts of this well-preserved temple, which is now home to

a golden spire. A brick wall surrounding its courtyard has become famous as the **Echo Wall**. If you stand facing the wall and speak to someone who is also standing by it, he or she will be able to hear every word at every point anywhere along the wall.

The three stone slabs in front of the stairs to the main temple are the **Echo Stones** (Sanyinshi), which produce another peculiar effect. If you stand on the first slab and clap your hands, you will hear a single echo. On the second step you will hear a double echo, and on the third, a triple.

Before the winter solstice ritual, the emperor would fast in the **Hall of Abstinence** (Zhaigong), which stands in the west of the temple complex. Then, by the first rays of the sun on the day of the solstice, he would offer sacrifices and prayers at the **Altar of Heaven** (Yuanqiu). This is the most spectacular of the city's imperial altars, consisting of a stone terrace of three levels surrounded by

two walls – an inner round one and an outer square one. The lowest level symbolises the Earth, the second, the world of human beings, and the last, Heaven. The altar is built from stone slabs, and its construction is based on the number nine and its multiples.

Walk along the central causeway that links the southern and northern buildings to reach the striking **Hall of Prayer for Good Harvests** (Qiniandian). The structure is built on a three-level marble terrace, each

Right: Temple of Heaven.

the Beijing Buddhist Society and a flock of brown-robed monks. China's last known eunuch, Sun Yaoting, was the temple's caretaker for 20 years until he died in 1996.

Taimiao (Imperial Ancestoral Temple)
Laodong Renmin Wenhuagong (Workers' Palace of Culture), Chang'an Jie, Dongcheng; daily 8am–4pm; entrance fee; subway: Tiananmen East; map p.136 B4

This venerable temple, dating from the 15th and 16th centuries, is just inside of the Tiananmen Gate. Five times a year the wooden ancestor tablets, upon which the names of the dead forefathers of the imperial family were recorded, were taken from the central hall in which they were kept to the southern hall, where the emperor paid his respects to his ancestors.

After 1949, Confucianism was seen as the embodiment of the feudal ways that Communism was trying to eradicate. Most Confucian temples throughout China were thus converted to other uses, or simply abandoned. Beginning in the late 1980s, there was an effort to revive some of the basic precepts of Confucianism, such as respect for authority and the elderly. But a real comeback seems impossible in the diverse and ever-evolving society that is modern China.

Gulou

The Confucius Temple (Kong Miao) and Imperial Academy (Guozijian)
13 Guozijian Jie, Dongcheng; tel: 8402 7224; daily 8.30am–5pm; entrance fee; subway: Yonghegong; map p.134 C3

The temple and the academy have been recently beautifully restored and are combined under one entrance ticket. Entering via the temple, in the main hall, the **Hall of Great Achievements** (Dachengdian), there are some of the musical instruments which were so important in Confucian ceremonies.

Scores of stone tablets recording names of successful scholars can be seen in the pavilions around the **Gate of the First Teacher** (Xianshimen).

Tradition dictated that on the right of a temple there should be an academy. So in the year 1306, during the Yuan dynasty, the Imperial Academy was founded as a school to teach the Chinese language to Mongol boys and Mongol to Chinese boys, as well as educating all pupils in all of the martial arts. Later, the academy

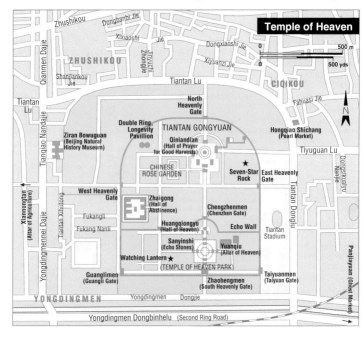

Right: the Lama Temple.

became a university churning out Confucian scholars.

The Lama Temple (Yonghegong)

12 Yonghegong Dajie, Dongcheng; tel: 6404 4499 ext. 251; daily 9am–4.30pm; entrance fee; subway: Yonghegong; map p.134 C3

Built in 1694, when it formed part of the city wall, it served as a residence for Yongzheng, the fourth son of Emperor Kangxi, before he ascended to the throne in 1722. Traditionally, the home of an heir to the throne would be turned into a temple after he had become ruler, or – as in this case – after his death.

Yongzheng's son and successor, Qianlong, sent for 300 Tibetan monks and 200 Chinese pupils and installed them in his father's old palace. It was considered one of the most notable centres of Lamaist Buddhism outside Tibet.

Coming from the south, enter the temple grounds through a gate. After crossing the gardens, you pass into the inner courtyard with its Bell and Drum Towers and

two pavilions with steles in them. To the north is the **Hall of the Celestial Kings** (Tianwangdian), with statues of the Maitreya Buddha and two guardian divinities.

Beyond the pavilion is a stone representation of the **World Mountain**, *Sumeru*. In the **Hall of Eternal Harmony** (Yonghedian) there are three statues of Buddha surrounded by 18 *Luohan*, one who has attained enlightenment. The buildings to the left and right of this inner courtyard house a mandala and valuable *thangka* – figures representing the founder of the Yellow Hat sect, Tsongkhapa. Crossing the next courtyard, you come to the **Hall of Eternal Protection** (Yongyoudian), with

statues of the Buddhas of longevity and medicine.

The halls to the left and right of the following courtyard contain, among other items, statues of Yab-Yum, a male and female divinity whose intimate sexual connection symbolises the cosmic unity of all opposites. This courtyard is bounded by the **Hall of the Wheel of Dharma** (Falundian), in the middle of which is a 6m- (20ft-) high statue of Tsongkhapa. Behind this statue is the monastery's treasure: a miniature mountain of sandalwood, with 500 *Luohan* figures of gold, silver, copper, iron and tin.

The fifth inner courtyard ends at the **Pavilion of Ten Thousand Happinesses**

Below: Lama and Confucius temples.

(Wanfuge). This contains a 25m- (80ft-) high Maitreya Buddha made from a single piece of sandalwood. The three-storey pavilion is linked by bridges to the two-storey side buildings that flank it.

The Embassy District

Dongyuemiao (Temple of the God of Tai Mountain)
141 Chaoyangmenwai Dajie, Chaoyang; tel: 6551 0151; daily 9am–4pm; entrance fee; subway: Chaoyangmen; map p.135 D1

The temple was built to honour the highest celestial ruler of the Tai Mountain, one of the five Daoist Holy Mountains in China. Founded by Zhang Daoling during the Yuan dynasty, this was once the largest of its kind in northern China. After 1949 the temple was converted into schools and administrative offices, but reopened in 1999 after comprehensive restoration work.

Off the main courtyard is the **Hall of Tai Mountain** (Daizongbaodian) – in the centre of which is a statue of the god of Tai Mountain, surrounded by his high-ranking servants. Elsewhere are hundreds of other Daoist deities, dedicated to a wide variety of moral and spiritual codes – on controlling bullying and cheating, caring for animals and upholding piety.

Zhihuasi (Temple of Perfect Wisdom)
Lumicang Hutong, Nanxiaojie, Dongcheng; tel: 6525 0072; daily 9am–4pm; entrance fee; subway:Chaoyangmen; map p.135 D1

This temple was built as a family shrine by a eunuch named Wang Zhen in 1443, during the Ming dynasty, but closed six years later when Wang was executed, after which it became imperial property. Wood blocks used for printing the 'Grand Collection of Buddhist Scriptures' are kept here. You can also catch a performance by the **Ancient Music Centre**.

SEE ALSO MUSIC, DANCE AND THEATRE, P.78

Western Beijing

Baitasi (Temple of the White Pagoda)
171 Fuchengmennei Dajie,

During the Cultural Revolution, the monastery was closed, with parts of it converted into a shoe factory. Red Guards took over the complex, but they were forbidden to destroy or plunder it by order of Zhou Enlai. In spite of this, many monks were ill-treated and sent away to do manual labour in the countryside. In the early 1980s, the monastery was reopened and completely restored.

Xicheng; tel: 6613 3317; daily 9am–4.30pm; entrance fee; subway: Fuchengmen; map p.133 D1

The temple is well known for its 51m white dagoba (a Tibetan-style shrine), which dates from 1279; it is larger and older than the similar structure in Beihai Park.

Its top is adorned by an engraved copper canopy, from which little bells hang, moving in the wind in order to drive away evil spirits. In the fourth hall there are sculptures of the three Buddhas and two Buddha pupils, as well as some *thangka*, or Tibetan scroll pictures.

Baiyunguan (Temple of the White Cloud)
6 Baiyunguan Jie; Xuanwu; tel: 6346 3531; daily 8.30am–4pm; entrance fee; subway: Nanlishi Lu; map p.138 C3

The temple site dates from the Tang dynasty (although the building itself dates from the Ming) and is the centre of the Daoist Dragon Gate sect. The complex contains several courtyards, the overall design being similar to Buddhist temples in that it faces south and its structures lie one behind the other along a straight line. Pass through the entrance gate into the first courtyard; the main attraction here is the pair of gong-like copper

Left: Buddhist paraphernalia.

coins with a bell in the centre suspended on strings. The idea is to throw (normal-sized) coins from the bridge – hitting the bell means good luck. Other ways to bring luck involve touching animal motifs and figures – the stone monkey at the entrance gate, or the bronze donkey in a western court-yard – or rubbing the belly on the large bronze statue of Wen Cheng, the scholar-deity in one of the western courtyards.

In the centre of the fur-thest courtyard is the **Hall of the Four Celestial Emper-ors**, and on its upper floor is the **Hall of the Three Puri-ties**. Daoist manuscripts are kept here in a compendium similar to those found in Buddhist temples.

Fayuansi (Temple of the Source of Buddhist Teaching)
Jiaozi Hutong, 7 Fayuansi Qian-jie, Xuanwu; tel: 6353 3966; Thur–Tue 8.30am–4pm; entrance fee; subway: taxi from Changchunjie; map p.139 D2
The oldest temple in the inner city of Beijing was completed in 696. The temple houses the Buddhist Academy, which is devoted to the

> Daoist temples use obvious symbolic motifs more frequently in their decoration than Buddhist temples. Common designs include the *Lingzhi* mushroom (which is supposed to prolong life), Daoist immortals, cranes and the eight trigrams from the Book of Changes.

teaching and study of Bud-dhism, and trains young monks for four to five years before they can enter other monasteries in China. Enter through **Shanmen**, the Mountain Gate. In the first temple courtyard is the **Hall of the Celestial Kings** (Tian-wangdian). The Celestial Kings rule the four points of the compass and can keep away all evil spirits and the enemies of Buddhism. Enthroned in the middle of the hall is a *Milefo*, a laugh-ing, fat-bellied Buddha, who encourages the faithful to 'come in, follow me on the way to release in nirvana'.

The main hall of the temple, the **Hall of Heroes** (Daxiongbaodian) is reached by crossing a garden with a bronze cauldron and stone steles. Behind that is the **Hall of a Thousand Buddhas**, with a 5m- (15ft-) high sculp-

ture dating back to the Ming dynasty, showing the Buddhas of the five points of the compass.

Guangjisi (Temple of Universal Rescue)
Fuchengmennei Dajie (opposite the Geological Museum), Xicheng; tel: 6616 0907; daily 9am–4.30pm; subway: Fuchengmen; map p.133 D2
The design of this temple follows the classic Buddhist architectural plan. In the third hall, the **Hall of Guanyin**, is a thousand-armed statue of the goddess of mercy, gilded during the Qing period. A copper Guanyin figure and a Guanyin on a lotus blossom dating from the Ming period are also on view in the hall.

Lidai Diwang Miao (Temple of Past Emperors)
Fuchengmennei Daijie, Xicheng; tel: 6616 1141; daily 9am–4pm; entrance fee; subway: Fucheng-men; map p.133 D1
Strictly speaking not a temple – you won't find any Buddha statues or Daoist deities inside – this ancient site was first constructed in 1530 as a place for emperors to make sacrifices to important histor-ical figures to help legitimise their own rule. After 1931 it became a school. It only opened to the public in 2004

Below: temple grounds are a community space used for games, music and teaching.

T

Left, right and below: Niu Jie Mosque.

'Diamond Throne Pagoda' style, and quite different from other temples in Beijing. Worth seeing above all else are the bas-reliefs on the outside, which depict Buddha figures, symbolic animals, lotus flowers, heavenly guardians, the wheel of Buddhist teaching, and other Buddhist symbols. Go up two flights of stairs to the terrace, where the bases of the pagodas are also adorned with reliefs.

Western Fringes

Biyunsi (Temple of the Azure Clouds)

Fragrant Hills Park, Haidian; tel: 6259 1155 ext. 470; daily 8am–5pm; entrance fee; subway: taxi from Xizhimen; map p.24

This 600-year-old temple is made up of four great halls, the innermost being the memorial hall for Sun Yat-sen. Here lies an empty coffin, a gift from the Soviet Union, which could not be used because it did not arrive until two weeks after the funeral.

To the left of the main entrance of the hall, letters and manuscripts left by Sun Yat-sen are on display.

after a major renovation. There's not a great deal to see inside except a spirit wall and stone steles.

Niu Jie Mosque

88 Niu Jie, Xuanwu; tel: 6353 2564; daily 9am–5pm; entrance fee; subway: taxi from Changchun Jie; map p.139 D2

The mosque was built in 966 in the style of a Buddhist temple, after the Islamic faith had spread into China during the Tang dynasty. Right behind the main entrance is a hexagonal building, the **Tower for Observing the Moon** (Wangyuelou). Beyond the tower is the main prayer hall. In the little courtyard garden that runs east is the tombstone – with an Arabic inscription – of the founder of the mosque.

North Cathedral (Beitang or Xishiku)

33 Xishiku Dajie, Xicheng; tel: 6617 5198; subway: Fuchengmen; map p.133 E1

This pretty cathedral, which sometimes looks purple in sunlight, was built by Jesuits in 1889. It is best known for its role in the frenzied Boxer Rebellion of 1900. The Boxers laid siege to the cathedral for seven weeks. The siege was finally ended by the intervention of Japanese soldiers. The church survived, only to be shut

down and looted during the Cultural Revolution. It was restored, and today has a sizeable congregation made up of Catholics of the Patriotic Church.

The North

Wutasi (Temple of Five Pagodas)

Baishiqiao, Haidian; tel: 6217 3543; daily 8am–4pm; entrance fee (Wed free); subway: Xizhimen; map p.132 B3

This temple dates back to the 15th-century reign of the Ming emperor Yongle. It was restored during Qianlong's reign but devastated by European troops in 1860 and again in 1900. The building, with five small pagodas standing on a massive square base, is in what is known in Buddhism as the

Beyond the memorial hall is the pagoda courtyard. The marble **Diamond Throne Pagoda** (Jingangbaozuota) was built in 1748 under the rule of Emperor Qianlong, and is modelled on Wutasi in northwest Beijing *(see left)*. The pagoda itself is 35m (115ft) high, and its base is adorned with numerous statues of Buddha.

Jietaisi (Ordination Terrace Temple)
Ma'an Shan, Mentougou;
tel: 6980 2645; daily 8am–5pm;
entrance fee; subway: taxi from Pingguoyuan; map p.24
This imposing temple dates from 622 and owes its name to the three-level stone terraces which were surrounded by statues and upon which the dedication ceremony of monks took place. The main hall is the **Daxiongbaodian**, and beyond it is the **Thousand Buddhas Pavilion**. Steles with Buddhist inscriptions dating from the Liao and Yuan dynasties can be seen in front of the Mingwang Hall. There is no longer much to be seen inside the halls, but it is worthwhile taking a walk to enjoy the temple grounds with their old pine trees.

Tanzhesi (Temple of the Poor and the Mulberry Tree)
Tanzhe shan, Mentougou;
tel: 6086 1699; daily 8am–5pm;
entrance fee; subway: taxi from Pingguoyuan; map p.24
Tanzhesi was built between AD 265 and 316 on terraces carved in dense woods – both Buddhists and Daoists traditionally withdraw to such beautiful places where they can meditate undisturbed. The temple is made up of three parts set along a north–south line across the hill slope. Enter following the central axis from the south, through the **Gate of Honour** and the adjoining Mountain Gate. The path is lined by picturesquely gnarled old pine trees. Beyond the Mountain Gate, one behind the other, are the **Hall of the Celestial Kings** (Tianwangdian), the **Daxiongbaodian Hall** (the main hall), the **Zhaitang Hall** and the **Piluge Pavilion**, dedicated to the Buddha Vairocana. Above the main hall are legendary beasts, sons of the Dragon King, who are supposed to

have captured a monk and chained him to the roof. There is a great view of Tanzhesi and its surroundings from here, the highest point in the grounds.

Take the western path from here and look into the **Temple of Guanyin**, where you can see the Paving Stone of Beizhuan. The path continues to the **Temple of the Dragon King** and the **Temple of the Founding Father**. In the eastern part of the grounds are a white dagoba dating from 1427, two groups of 12th-century pagodas, a bamboo grove and the **Pavilion of the Moving Cup** (Liubeige), where Qianlong stayed during his visits to the temple.

Wofosi (Temple of the Reclining Buddha)
Wofosi Lu, Botanical Gardens, Haidian; tel: 6259 1283; daily 8am–4pm; entrance fee; subway: taxi from Xizhimen; map p.24
This temple dates from the Tang dynasty. The 54-tonne, 5m (15ft) bronze Buddha is of indeterminate age, although experts have expressed doubts that it is the original statue. The original statue was apparently built by 7,000 slaves. Surrounding the Buddha are transcendental Bodhisattvas. Beyond the temple is the Cherry Ravine (Yingtaogou), a romantic spot.

> China's Communist Party likes to boast that its people enjoy complete freedom of religion. The real truth is there are only five authorised religions in China – Buddhism, Daoism, Islam, Catholicism and Protestantism. And each one has to belong to a state-affiliated organisation. China's State Catholic Church does not recognise the Vatican.

Transport

A major modernisation of the capital's transport systems is proving to be both Beijing's blessing and blight. The improved logistics – an expanded Normon Foster-designed airport, an extended subway network and huge investment in the road systems – mean it is generally cheaper and easier to get to and around the city. But with car ownership growing at the average rate of 1,000 new vehicles a day, pollution and congestion has become, at times, unbearable. While the armies of cyclists on their Flying Pigeons are now long gone, the city remains bicycle-friendly, with wide cycle lanes and quiet hutong ideal for pedalling.

Getting There

BY AIR

From London flight time is around 10 hours. **British Airways** and **Air China** are the only two airlines that offer direct flights. From North America, flights from the west coast take around 13 hours, from the east coast 18 to 20 hours. **Air China** is often the cheapest option.

Air China
Tel: 800 400 8100 999;
www.airchina.com.cn
British Airways
Tel: 400 650 0073;
www.britishairways.com

BY RAIL

An exciting way to travel between Beijing and Europe, at least for those with plenty of time, is to take the Trans-Siberian railway. Trains leave from Beijing Zhan, the start of a five-day (via Mongolia) or six-day (via Northeast China) journey to Moscow.

It takes about 24 hours by sleeper train from Hong Kong to Beijing; there are also two trains weekly from Vietnam (Hanoi) to Beijing.

BY SEA

The nearest port to Beijing is in Tianjin, an hour away by train. There are ferry services between Tianjin and the South Korean port of Incheon, and Kobe in Japan. For marine connections with South Korea see www.seoul searching.com/transportation/boat. And for schedules from Japan try www.seejapan.co.uk.

To and From the Airport

Beijing Capital International Airport is 30km (19 miles) from the city.

TAXI

The journey takes about 30 minutes, but allow an hour or more at peak hours. A fare into town, including the RMB10 toll, will average RMB100. Ignore the touts and queue up at the designated taxi lines.

AIRPORT BUS

The efficient airport coach costs RMB16. Destinations include Xidan, the Lufthansa Centre and the Beijing International Hotel, north of Beijing Zhan Station.

SUBWAY

The Airport Extension, a 28km (17 mile) high-speed rail link between Terminals 2 and 3 and Dongzhimen Station downtown, is due to open in 2008. Journey time is estimated at 15–17 minutes, the ticket price around RMB20.

Getting Around

Beijing has five main ring roads (the Second, Third, Fourth, Fifth and Sixth). Most other main roads run north–south or east–west, making it easy to navigate through the city. Main streets are commonly divided in terms of *bei* (north), *nan* (south), *xi* (west) and *dong* (east); and in terms of *nei* (inside) and *wai* (out-

Beijing has poured billions of dollars into expanding its airport. The new Norman Foster-designed **Terminal 3** is where most international airlines fly into. The expansion means Beijing's airport is now one of the world's five largest. Terminal 3 alone is bigger than all five Heathrow terminals combined.

Left: vintage wheels.

accessible. A direct underground shuttle linking the two is expected by the Olympics.
Beijing Station
Beijing Zhanjie, Dongcheng; tel: 5182 1114; subway: Beijing Zhan; map p.137 C3
Beijing West Railway Station
Lianhuachi Donglu, Fengtai; tel: 5182 6253; subway: taxi from Muxidi

TAXIS
A journey costs RMB2 per km after the initial 3km (2 miles), still cheap by Western standards. The flagfall is RMB10. Between 11pm and 5am, the basic fare and the cost per km are higher. Unless it is raining or rush hour, you should be able to flag down a cab within a couple of minutes. All taxis are metered, and drivers are reliable at using them.

   Drivers speak little English, so carrying Chinese name cards for hotels, restaurants, shops or other destinations can be useful for showing where you want to go. Always carry enough change, since taxi drivers are often unable to change large bills.

CAR RENTAL
Foreigners need a local licence to drive in China. More practical is to hire a car with a driver. This can be done through most travel agencies and hotels, or just by flagging down a taxi and negotiating.
Beijing Beiqi Taxi
Tel: 8677 5998;
www.beiqitaxi.com.cn
A Volkswagen Jetta costs RMB400 per day with a driver.

side) the Second Ring Road. The words *jie*, *dajie*, *lu* and *men*, which you'll find on all maps, mean street, avenue, road and gate respectively.

BICYCLES
If you have steady nerves, strong legs and a high tolerance for pushy car drivers, cycling is a great way to get around. Most guesthouses rent bicycles for around RMB30 a day. Lock your bicycles at guarded lots. Parking fees are at most 5 mao. If you want to experience a cyclist's pace but don't feel up to cycling yourself, pedicabs can be hired near tourist sites.

BOATS
A boat service operates from two points in Western Beijing to the New Summer Palace, along the Long River. Departures are hourly in the summer, journey time is one hour.

BUSES
The bus network is comprehensive and operates from 5am to 11pm. Most rides only cost around RMB1. Journeys are slow and crowded .

SUBWAY
Beijing's subway system is fast and cheap. Journeys cost a flat-rate RMB2, and there are trains every few minutes from 5.30am until 11pm. It is easy to find your way around: signs and announcements are bilingual. Buy your ticket from the ticket-office window.

RAIL
Beijing has two main railway stations: **Beijing Zhan** (Beijing Station) and **Beijing Xi Zhan** (Beijing West Station). The former is centrally located and connected to the subway system, the latter is in the southwestern suburbs and less

Left: Beijing subway.

Walks and Views

Get above the construction dust and Beijing is a sight to behold. Some of the newest skyscrapers offer sweeping bird's-eye views of a city in the making. While not as soaring, the hills and towers in the centre of the city award good views of the ancient buildings of imperial Beijing from above. A nose around the old quarters – the hutong areas and the colonial district – offer a unique atmosphere and insight into the capital's past. While on clear days, from some of the peaks in the western fringes, such as Fragrant Hill, you can see the city in miniature on the horizon.

The Foreign Legation Quarter

Subway: Wangfujing;
map p.136 B4

The villas and mansions of the foreign legation quarter are often overlooked by tourists, but a stroll around these streets is a unique experience; there are few other examples of colonial architecture in Beijing.

Towards the northern end of Taijichang Dajie, the grand red-brick towers of the former **Italian Legation** are now the headquarters of the Chinese People's Friendship Association. Down the hutong to the east is the grey-and-white Greek-temple-facade entrance to the **Austro-Hungarian Legation**, now housing the Institute of International Studies. Back on Taijichang is the grey-blue-walled **Peking Club**. Built in 1902, complete with tennis courts and a swimming pool, this is the exclusive haunt of high-ranking Chinese Communist Party officials.

Further south, on the corner of Dongjiaomin Xiang and

partly hidden by a newer building, is **St Michael's** Catholic Church *(see p.118)*, built by the French Vincentian Fathers in 1902. The rear entrance to the expansive grounds of the former **Belgian Legation** is across the street. It now functions as a state guesthouse. Nearby is the old **French Legation**, once the Beijing residence of the late Sihanouk, king of Cambodia, distinguished by an imposing grey gate with red doors and two large stone lions standing guard.

On the corner of Dongjiaomin Xiang and

Left: the Italian legation.

Zhengyi Lu is the large red-and-white-brick building of the **Yokohama Specie Bank**, where Cixi supposedly took out a loan. Looking south is the site of the **Grand Hôtel des Wagon-Lits**, which was the fashionable place to stay, and was close to the old railway station outside the wall. In the southwest corner, the former **American Legation** is being transformed into a high-end dining and entertainment zone.

Head north on Zhengyi Lu, an attractive street with shady parkland, although 100 years ago it would have been running with sewage from the Forbidden City, and you will come to an impressive red-towered gate. This is the **Japanese Legation**, and it was here that the Chinese were forced to accept the infamous 'Twenty-One Demands' on 7 May 1915, whereby the Japanese obtained special rights over Manchuria. It is now the offices of the Beijing Municipal People's Government.

Left: the ultimate walk.

Wall is not merely to see one of the Wonders of the World; for many visitors it is the breathtaking vista from its crumbling ramparts and the opportunities for hiking through rugged terrain. A popular hike is the rather demanding four-hour scramble between **Simatai** and **Jinshanling**. Because of the damage wrought by tourists, patches of the Wall, dubbed the 'wild wall', are now off limits. British researcher and Great Wall boffin William Lindesay, who was the first foreigner to walk its full length back in 1987, melds education and conservation with his thoughtful 'wild wall' trips – he works for the Beijing Administrative Bureau for Cultural Relics, so he has permission.
See www.wildwall.com.

SEE ALSO THE GREAT WALL, P.26–7

A visit to Beijing would not be complete with a walk around the hutong (see p.68–9). It is easy to get lost in the maze of grey-walled Ming-dynasty lanes, but despite a few dead ends, you will inevitably emerge onto a main road sooner or later. The web of hutong around Houhai and the Drum and Bell Towers are the most atmospheric. They have the advantage of offering a good chance of stumbling across a little café or restaurant.

Almost opposite is the old **British Legation**. Previously a prince's palace, this building was the city's largest foreign legation. It is now owned by the police.

Fragrant Hills

The Fragrant Hills are an easy one-hour taxi ride out of the city and are a gentler hiking experience than the Great Wall. The main peak itself offers a great view of the capital and nearby temple-dotted wooded slopes,

provided the pollution levels are low. In the south of the park and past the remains of the once massive **Xiangshan Temple** (destroyed in 1860) that rose over six levels, there is the remote **Twin Peaks Villa** (Shuang Qing Shanzhuang) and the **Pavilion Halfway up the Hill** (Banshanting). Here, a small tower has been restored, and from it you get a good view of the park.

The Great Wall

The attraction of the Great

Right: Fragrant Hills Park.

The ambitious skyscrapers of the Central Business District promise magnificent views of the capital. Sneak into the **Park Hyatt** (see p.66) in the Yintai Centre or the **China World Trade Centre Tower 3** (see p.18) for the most elevated views. The view from the **Pavilion of Everlasting Spring** in Jingshan (Coal Hill) (see p.98–9) is superb, as is the view from the **White Dagoba** in Beihai Park (see p.96). At the top of the near-vertical flight of steps in the Drum Tower you will be rewarded with a good view over Houhai Lake. Dozens of bars and restaurants boast appealing views, too many to list here. **Ken de Rouge** restaurant (see p.102) and **East Shore Live Jazz Café** (see p.78–9) have a window on Houhai Lake.

Atlas

The following streetplan of Beijing makes it easy to find the attractions listed in our A–Z section. A selective index to streets and sights will help you find other locations throughout the city

Map Legend

═══	Motorway	Ⓓ	Metro Station
───	Dual carriageway	🚌	Bus station
▨▨▨	Ring road	✈	Airport
──	Main road	❶	Tourist information
──	Minor road	★	Sight of interest
══	Footpath	🏴	Beach
▬▬▬	Railway	⚲	Buddhist temple
▨	Pedestrian area	ψ	Hindu temple
▨	Notable building	🏯	Chinese temple
▨	Park	⊞	Cathedral / church
▨	Hotel	☾	Mosque
▨	Urban area	✡	Synagogue
▨	Non urban area	🧍	Statue / monument
✝ ✝	Cemetery	✚	Hospital

p132	p133	p134	p135
p138	p139	p136	p137

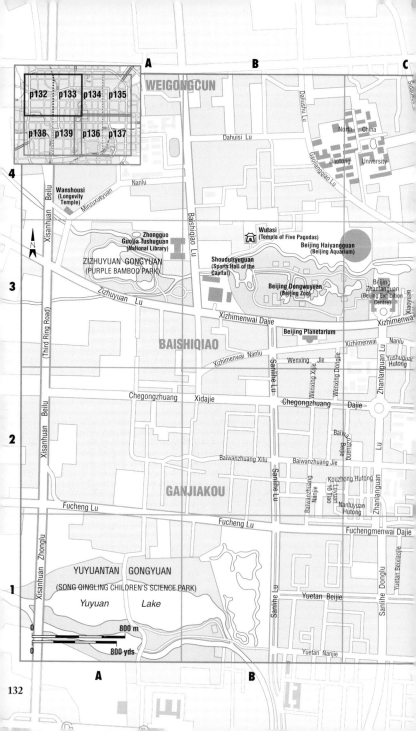

WEIGONGCUN

p132 p133 p134 p135

p138 p139 p136 p137

4

Dahuishu Lu

Dahuisi Lu

North China

Jiaotong University

Nanlu

Wanshousi
(Longevity
Temple)

Minzuxueyuan

Xisanhuan Beilu

Baishiqiao Lu

Wutasi
(Temple of Five Pagodas)

Beijing Haiyangguan
(Beijing Aquarium)

Zhongguo
Guojia Tushuguan
(National Library)

Shoudutiyuguan
(Sports Hall of the
Capital)

ZIZHUYUAN GONGYUAN
(PURPLE BAMBOO PARK)

Beijing Dongwuyuan
(Beijing Zoo)

Beijing
Zhanlanguan
(Beijing Exhibition
Centre)

Xiaoyojie

3

Zizhuyuan Lu

Xizhimenwai Dajie

Xizhimenwai

(Third Ring Road)

BAISHIQIAO

Beijing Planetarium

Nanlu

Xizhimenwai

Zhanlanguan Lu

Yushuguan
Hutong

Xizhimenwai Nanlu

Wenxing Jie

Sanlihe Lu

Wenxing Xijie

Wenxing Dongjie

Chegongzhuang Xidajie

Chegongzhuang Dajie

Xisanhuan Beilu

2

Baiwanzhuang Xilu

Baiwanzhuang Jie

Sanlihe Lu

Baiwanzhuang Nanjie

Baiwanzhuang Beijie

Lu

Zhanlanguan

GANJIAKOU

Kouzhong Hutong

Lu Tou 10

Nantuyuan
Hutong

Nantuyuan
Hutong

Fucheng Lu

Fucheng Lu

Fuchengmenwai Dajie

Xisanhuan Zhonglu

Sanlihe Lu

Sanlihe Donglu

Yuetan Beixiaojie

1

YUYUANTAN GONGYUAN

(SONG QINGLING CHILDREN'S SCIENCE PARK)

Yuyuan Lake

Yuetan Beijie

0 ____ 800 m

0 ____ 800 yds

Yuetan Nanjie

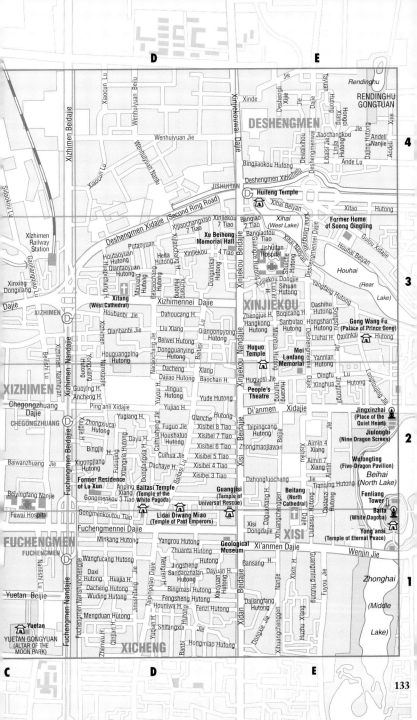

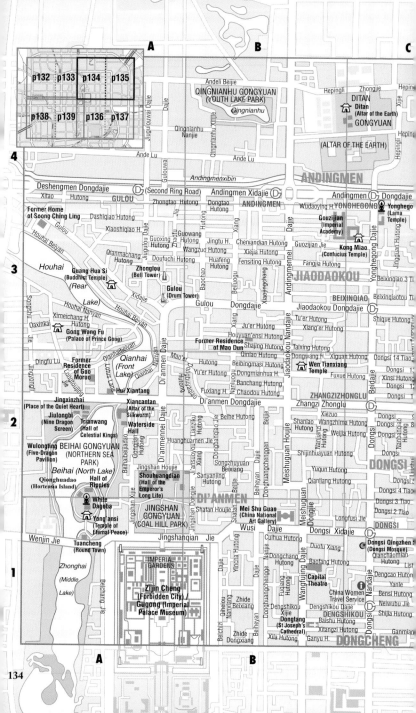

A B C

4

Andeli Beijie

QINGNIANHU GONGYUAN
(YOUTH LAKE PARK)

Qingnianhu

Hepingli Zhongjie Hepingli

DITAN
Ditan (Altar of the Earth)
GONGYUAN

(ALTAR OF THE EARTH)

Hepingli

Qingnianhu Nanjie

Qingnianhu Xililu

Ande Lu

Ande Lu

Andingmenxibin (Second Ring Road)

Deshengmen Dongdajie GULOU (Second Ring Road) Andingmen Xidajie Andingmen Andingmen Dongdajie

Xitao Hutong Zhongtao Hutong Dongtao Hutong ANDINGMEN

Wudaoying H. YONGHEGONG
Yonghego
(Lama Temple)

Former Home of Soong Ching Ling Dashiqiao Hutong Guoxing Hutong Guowang Hutong Jingtu H. Chenandian Hutong Gouzijian (Imperial Academy) Yonghegong Dajie

Xiaoshiqiao H. Doufuchi Hutong Wangzuo Hutong Xieja Hutong Guozijian Jie

Houhai Beiyan Gulou Qianmachang Hutong Huafeng Hutong Fensiting Hutong Kong Miao (Confucius Temple)

Houhai Zhonglou (Bell Tower) Fangjia Hutong

Guang Hua Si (Buddhist Temple) (Rear) Baochao JIAODAOKOU Beixinqiao 3 Ti

Houhai Nanyan Xidajie Gulou Dongdajie Xiaojingchang Beixinqiao

Ximeichang H. Houhai Beiyan Beiluogu Jiaodaokou Dongdajie Beixinqiaotou Ti

Daxinka Hutong Ju'er Hutong Tu'er Hutong Shique Hutong

Gong Wang Fu (Palace of Prince Gong) Houyuan'ensi Hutong Xiang'er Hutong Dongsi 14 Tiao

Former Residence of Mao Dun Shajing Hutong Taixing Hutong Xinsi Hutong Dongsi 1

Dingfu Lu Qianhai (Front Lake) Qinlao Hutong Dongwang H. Xiguan Hutong Dongsi 1

Former Residence of Guo Moruo Hui Xiantang Beibingmasi Hutong Wen Tianxiang Temple Fuxue Hutong Dongsi 1

Yu'er Hutong Dongmianhua H. ZHANGZIZHONGLU

Banchang Hutong Dongsi

Xiancantan (Altar of the Silkworm) Fuxiang H. Chaodou Hutong Zhangzi Zhonglu Dongsi 8

Jingxinzhai (Place of the Quiet Heart) Di'anmen Dongdajie Xiezuo Dongsi

Jiulongbi (Nine Dragon Screen) Waterside Hall Beihe Hutong Shanlao Wangzhima Hutong Dongsi 5

Trianwang (Hall of Celestial Kings) Huanghuamen Jie Nanjianzi Weija Hutong Dongsi 6

Wulongting (Five-Dragon Pavilion) BEIHAI GONGYUAN (NORTHERN SEA PARK) Shijinhuayuan Hutong Dongsi

Qionghuadao (Hortensa Island) Hall of Ripples Songzhuyuan Hutong Yuqun Hutong Dongsi

White Dageba Sanyanjing Hutong Qianliang Hutong Dongsi 4 Tiao

Yong'ansi (Temple of Eternal Peace) Shouhuangdian (Hall of the Emperor's Long Life) Dongsi 3 Tiao

Tuancheng (Round Town) JINGSHAN GONGYUAN (COAL HILL PARK) Shatan Houjie Mei Shu Guan (China National Art Gallery) Dongsi 2 Tiao DONGSI

Wenjin Jie DI'ANMEN Wusi Dajie Dongsi Xidajie Longfusi Jie

Zhonghai (Middle Lake) Jingshanqian Jie Culhua Hutong Duofu Xiang Dongsi Qingzhen (Dongsi Mosque)

IMPERIAL GARDENS Dongchang Hutong Baofang Hutong Qianchaomian Hutong

Zijin Cheng (Forbidden City) / Gugong (Imperial Palace Museum) Fuqiang Hutong Capital Theatre China Women Travel Service Dengcao Hutong Yanle

Dengshikou Xijie Dongtang (St Joseph's Cathedral) Baishu Hutong Bensi Hutong Neiwubu Jie

Zhide Dongxiang Xila Hutong Ganyu H. DENGSHIKOU Xitangzi Hutong Shijia Hutong

Ganmian
DONGCHENG

A B

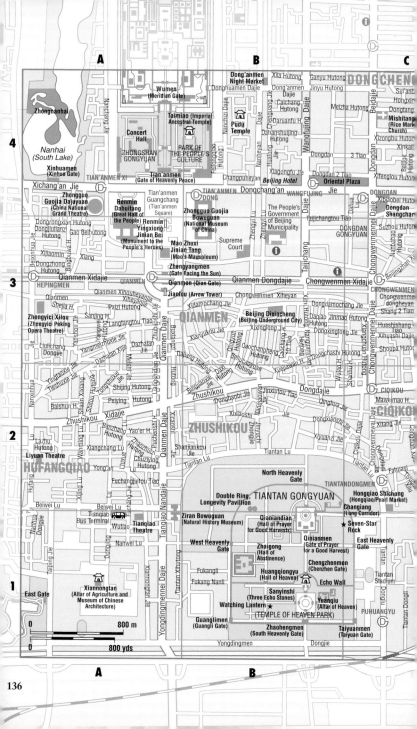

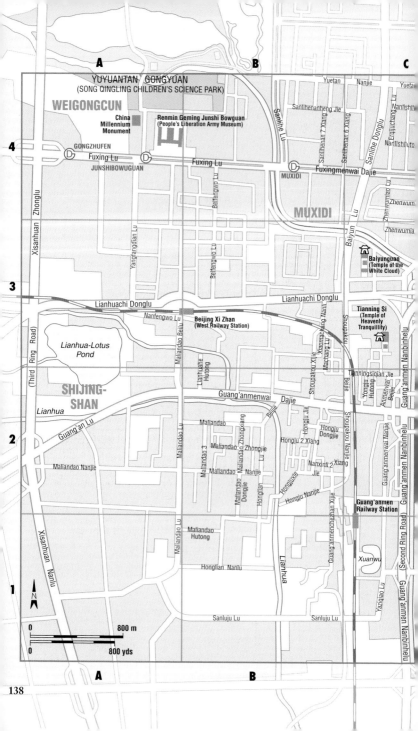

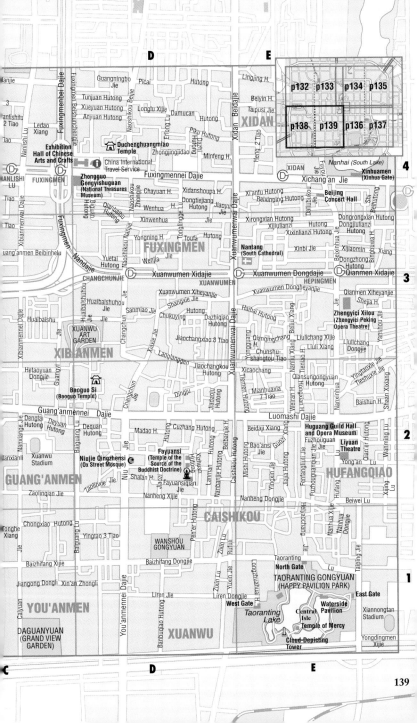

D   E

Wanjie
Guangningbo   Picai
Jie   Hutong
Tunjuan Hutong
antishilu   Ledao   Naoshikou Beijie   Longfu Xijie   Damucan
2 Tiao   Lang   Erlong Lu   Piku Hutong
Nanlishilu   Anyuan Hutong   Hutong
Tiao
Exhibition   🏛 Duchenghuangmiao   Zhongjingjiedao
Hall of Chinese   Temple   Minfeng H.
Arts and Crafts   ℹ️ China International
Travel Service

Lingjing H.
Belyin H.
Taipusi Jie   p132 p133   p134 p135

XIDAN

p138 p139   p136 p137

Nanhai (South Lake)

D ANLISHI D FUXINGMEN   XIDAN   Xinhuamen
   LU   (Xinhua Gate)
Tiao
Zhongguo   Fuxingmennei Dajie   Xichang'an Jie
Tiao   Gongyishuguan
(National Treasures
Museum)   Qianbaidu   Xidanshoupa H.   Xi'anfu Hutong   Beijing
Naoshikou   Chayuan H.   Dongtiejiang   Beixinping Hutong   Concert Hall
Zhongjie   Xinwenhua   Jiaoyu   Jie   Dongrongxian Hutong
Biguan   Toufa   Xirongxian Hutong   Dongjiulianzi
Hutong   Yongning H.   Hutong   Xijiulianzi   Hutong   Hutong
FUXINGMEN   Jie   Nantang   Xixinlianzi Hutong   Xijiaomin
Yuetai   (South Cathedral)   Xinbi Jie   Hutong
Hutong   Wenjia   Jie   Dongzhong
D   Wenla   Xuanwumen Dongdajie D Hutong Qianmen Xidajie
CHANGCHUNJIE   Xuanwumen Xidajie   D   D
XUANWUMEN   HEPINGMEN
Xuanwumen Xiheyanjie   Xuanwumen Dongheyanjie   Qianmen Xiheyanjie
Huaibaishuhou   Shangxie Jie   Shejia H.
Jie   Sanmiao Jie   Hutong   Dazhiqiao   Haibai Hutong   Zhengyici Xilou
XUANWU   Changchun   Chukuying   Hutong   (Zhengyici Peking
ART GARDEN   Dongguang   Opera Theatre)
Xiajie   Jiaochangxiao 8 Tiao   Qianqingchang   Liulichang Xijie
XIBIANMEN   Laoqianggen   Chunshu-   Liuli Xiang   Liulichang
Hetaoyuan   Jiaochangkou   shangtou Tiao   Dongjie
Dongjie   Hutong   Xicaochang   Qiansungongyuan
Baoguo Si 🏛   Mianhuaxia   Hutong   Yingtaoxie Jie
(Baoguo Temple)   Dingjiu   7 Tiao   Nanxinhua   Tieshuxie Jie
Guang'anmennei Dajie   Jiadaou   Baishun H. Shaan Xixiang

Denglai   Deyuan   Cuzhang Hutong   Beidaji Xiang   Huguang Guild Hall
Nanxiangxi Hutong Hutong   Madao H.   Bao'ansi   and Opera Museum
Jianxianli Xianxiang   Dequan   Hutong   Jie   Fuzhouguan   Liyuan
Xuanwu   Hutong   Baiguang Lanman   Bangzarjie H.   Xiaojie   Theatre
Stadium   Hutong   Yong'an Lu
GUANG'ANMEN   Niujie Qingzhensi ☪️ Fayuansi   Caishikou Hutong   HUFANGQIAO
Zhaolinqiao Jie   (Ox Street Mosque) (Temple of the   Mishi Hutong
Chongxiao Hutong   Shalan H. Source of the   Nanheng Dongjie   Beiwei Lu
Tonghe   Buddhist Doctrine)
Xiang   Yingtao 3 Tiao   Ja Fayuansiqian
Baiguang   Jie Nanheng Xijie   CAISHIKOU
Baizhifang Xijie   Perter Hutong   Jie
Jiangong Dongli Xin'an Zhongli   WANSHOU   Zizhu Lu
YOU'ANMEN   Baizhifang Dongjie   GONGYUAN   Taoranting
DAGUANYUAN   Liren Jie   Yuxin Jie   North Gate
(GRAND VIEW   Liren Dongjie   TAORANTING GONGYUAN
GARDEN)   You'anmennei Dajie   West Gate   (HAPPY PAVILION PARK) East Gate
Caiyuan   Banbuqiao Hutong   Taoranting   Waterside   Xiannongtan
XUANWU   Lake   Central   Pavilion   Stadium
Temple of Mercy   Isle
Cloud-Depicting   Yongdingmen
Tower   Xijie

C   D   E

139

Index

Insight Smart Guide: Beijing
Written by: Dinah Gardner
Edited by: Jason Mitchell
Proofread and indexed by: Neil Titman

All pictures © APA/Ming Tang-Evans,
Richard and Abe Nowitz except; AKG
51B; Alamy 63B; Corbis 43B, 84M;
Eyevine 48, 57; Getty 49B, 56B, 73T,
115T; Hemis 62T, 63T, 67T; Imagine
China 7T, 49T, 59B, 79T; Rex 50T;
Picture Manager: Steven Lawrence
Maps: Neal Jordan-Caws
Series Editor: Jason Mitchell
Series Concept: Maria Lord

First Edition 2008
© 2008 Apa Publications GmbH & Co.
Verlag KG Singapore Branch, Singapore.

Printed in Singapore by Insight Print
Services (Pte) Ltd

Worldwide distribution enquiries:
Apa Publications GmbH & Co. Verlag KG
(Singapore Branch) 38 Joo Koon Road,
Singapore 628990; tel: (65) 6865 1600;
fax: (65) 6861 6438
Distributed in the UK and Ireland by:
GeoCenter International Ltd
Meridian House, Churchill Way West,
Basingstoke, Hampshire RG21 6YR;
tel: (44 1256) 817 987; fax: (44 1256)
817 988
Distributed in the United States by:
Langenscheidt Publishers, Inc.
36–36 33rd Street 4th Floor, Long Island
City, New York 11106; tel: (1 718) 784
0055; fax: (1 718) 784 0640l

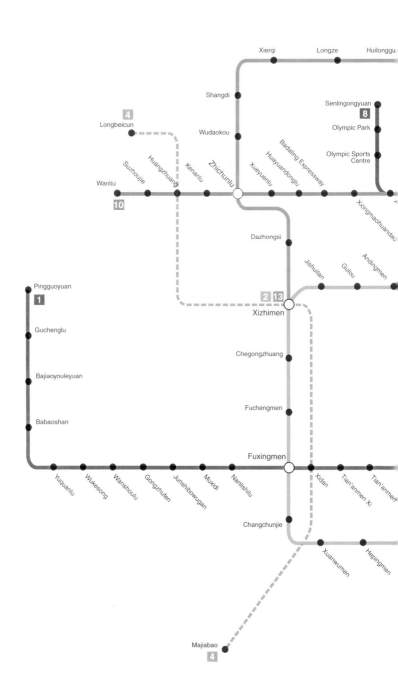